Alcohol ̄ive America

160201

Alcohol Problems in Native America:

The Untold Story of Resistance and Recovery--

The Truth About the Lie

Don L. Coyhis and William L. White

White Bison Inc.

An American Indian non Profit Organization
Colorado Springs, Colorado

Book design, layout, and editing by Richard Simonelli

ISBN 1-59975-229-8

1. Native American history   2. Addictions recovery   3. Native American studies   4. Community development

To order books:

White Bison, Inc.
6145 Lehman Drive, Suite 200
Colorado Springs, CO 80918-3440
(719) 548-1000 voice
(719) 548-9407 fax
toll-free 1-877-871-1495
website:
www.whitebison.org

This book is dedicated to the Indigenous People of North America who resisted, and who continue to resist the harm of oppression and colonization caused by alcohol and other drugs. We offer this book so that the People will continue to resist, recover, survive and thrive. We present this book so that from this time onward it shall be
a good day to live!

Cover Photo
Handsome Lake Preaching His Code in the Longhouse, by Ernest Smith, Seneca. 1930's.
Courtesy of Rochester Museum and Science Center, Rochester NY

Back-of-Book Photo
Journey Beyond the American Dream, by Adrian Larvie, Oglala Lakota/Sioux, 2002. Courtesy of the artist.

Acknowledgements

This book is more the product of a movement than the individual achievement of the authors. We have been honored to serve that movement and wish to acknowledge some of the individuals and organizations that have helped bring to life the story you are about to enter.

We honor the Native Elders who have nurtured the larger Wellbriety Movement and who inspired us to pursue work on this project. Particular thanks go to Joe Coyhis; Horace Axtell; Bill Iron Moccasin; Ozzie Williamson; Harold and Wanda Frogg; Ernie Turner; Rich Harrison and so many others. We cordially invite you, the reader, to inform White Bison, Inc. of other men and women in your own communities–both contemporary and historic–who have resisted the effects of alcohol and helped their people survive. Their names belong in future editions of this book.

We honor the Native leaders and communities, past and present, who make up the heart of this story. Their lives and their tenacious struggle to survive and develop as individuals, families, tribes and as a People sowed the seeds from which this book grew. We have drawn strength to work on this project from Native communities across North America and from our knowledge that healing movements are rising among Indigenous Peoples around the world. As we spoke of this project in our travels through Indian country, many people offered encouragement and shared historical details and sources. We are indebted to all who offered such support. Particular thanks go to Michael Sims, Kurt Kaupisch and Jack Gladstone who linked us to previously unknown resources.

We thank the scholars who have helped unravel the truths of Native Peoples' historical relationship with alcohol. We are particularly indebted to the work of Craig MacAndrew, Robert Edgerton, Dwight Heath, Peter Mancall, William Unrau, Hugh Dempsey and Richard Thatcher. The writings of Maria Yellow Horse Brave Heart and Patricia Morgan helped us frame this relationship within the larger context of historical trauma and the processes of colonization and decolonization (political sovereignty and cultural renewal). We also wish to acknowledge the scholars who have challenged the "Firewater Myths" that contribute to the stereotypes and misconstruction of Native alcohol problems. The studies of Joy Leland, Philip May, Dr. Joseph Westermeyer and Richard Thatcher are particularly noteworthy in their influence on this book. We especially acknowledge the work of Gene Thin Elk in Indian communities across North America. We are grateful for the critical reading and editorial comments of the first draft of this book by Candace Shelton and David Kagabitang.

We thank the institutions and librarians from across the country who helped us obtain the archival resources that helped us construct this the documentation of this story. We are particularly indebted to the many institutions, organizations and individuals who consented to the use of their photographic materials in this book. We welcome communications about those graphics we still need to acknowledge.

We would also like to thank Adele C. Smithers-Fornaci and the Christopher D. Smithers Foundation, Inc. for the financial support to print and distribute the first printing of this book to Native communities across North America.

CONTENTS

Part Four: The Lessons of History

The Red Road

"The Red Road is a holistic approach to mental, physical, spiritual and emotional wellness based on Native American healing concepts and traditions, having prayer as the basis of all healing. Native American psychology is essential in reaching the inner person (spirit) using specific sound, movement, and color. All these essences are present in the Medicine Wheel, which is innate to Native Americans. The traditions and values of the Native American People ensure balance by living these cultural traditions through the Red Road. Healing is a way of life for the Native American who understands and lives the cultural traditions and values." *

—Gene Thin Elk,
Lakota Nation

*Arbogast, D. (1995). *Wounded Warriors*. Omaha, NE: Little Turtle Publications. p. 319

Foreword

From Chickens to Eagles:
Discovery of the Red Road

We want to begin with a simple proposition—the proposition that the character of Indian People has been deformed by the sustained assault on Native cultures. To take our lands, non-Indian people had to convince us we were something other than what we were. To kill our ancestors and take our lands, they had to define us as something less than human. To colonize or exterminate a people, you must first define them as a weed. You must transform them from a person to a pestilence. Once objectified, they can be killed without thought or remorse. But this process is even more insidious. The ultimate evil inflicted on Indian people was teaching us to hate ourselves so deeply as a people that we began killing ourselves and killing each other.

Non-Indian invaders created a caricature of the Indian. They described us so often and so consistently over generations that we began to believe the lies ourselves and act in harmony with this view. A lie told a thousand times often becomes the truth to those who tell it, to those who hear it, and even to those the lie is about. We want to illustrate this truth by sharing with you a story about how deeply imbedded lies can shape who we are at a most fundamental level.

A Story About Chickens and Eagles

There was a farmer out in the forest and he heard gunshots. He walked to where the shots were fired and found on the ground two eagles lying there. Somebody shot both of those eagles. As he stood there, all of a sudden he heard a little noise and he looked up and there was a nest up above. You could hear little eagles in the nest. So he climbed up that tree and looked in the nest to find two little eaglets. He didn't know what to do so he put them in his pocket and climbed back down the tree and went back home. He was trying to figure out what he should do with the baby eagles so he said to himself, "I'll just put them in with the chickens." He took them out to the chicken coop and put those eagles there.

As time went on they grew a little bit and one day they were talking with each other in eagle language. And one said to the other, "You know, we're different. We don't look like them."

Then the other one said, "Don't be talking like that. We're chickens. I talked to some of those chickens and they told us that we're chickens. So don't be talking like that."

Time went on and they grew a little bit. Pretty soon one came back and said, "You know, we are really different."

The other said, "Just shut up! They taught us how to crow, we flap our wings like they do, we walk like they do, we do everything like they do. We're chickens."

Summer came and one of the eagles went walking down a path and kind of strayed away from the flock. As he got into the forest a little bit he began to hear laughter. It was a really hard, gut-barrel laughter. He looked up to see an owl sitting in a tree. So the eagle looked up at the owl and said, "What are you laughing at?"

The owl kept on laughing and he said, "I'm laughing because you're acting like a chicken. You're an eagle but you're acting just like a chicken."

But right away the eagle says, "No, I'm a chicken."

"No," said the owl, "you're an eagle!" The owl couldn't convince him so finally the owl flew down and landed by the eagle and he said, "I want you to get on my back and hang on." So he got on the back of that owl and the owl took off down the runway and made elevation and started riding the air currents. Pretty soon the owl was way up in the sky. He said to his passenger, the eagle, "This is you. You soar with the wind. You look way out. You can fly higher than anything."

The eagle is hanging on the owl and he's so scared of the height and he's saying, "No, I'm a chicken, I'm a chicken. Get me back down."

By then the owl is getting ready and he says, "I really hate to do this to you but I've got to do it." The owl just flipped over. The eagle went tumbling through the air and the owl dived down alongside the eagle and he said, "Spread your wings, spread your wings."

"I can't, I cant."

"Spread your wings!"

But pretty soon the eagle started to put out his wings and the wind started to catch them, and all of a sudden...all of a sudden, he just started soaring. He couldn't believe that he was soaring. He was just amazed.

After a while he landed and went back to the chicken coop and the other eagle was still sitting in there. He was trying to snag those chickens, and all that stuff. Making the moves and competing with the roosters, but the other eagle said, "Brother, come over here." He whispered into his ear and he said, "You know something, we're eagles, we're not chickens."

But then the other eagle got indignant and said, "Oh no! Don't you be talking like that. They trained us, they told us what we are. I can do it really good. I can be a chicken really good."

"No," the other eagle said, "that's not who we are." They argued a little bit and the one who had flown said, "I want you to come for a walk with me." He took his brother for a walk and met the owl, and together they put him on the owl and up they went, riding the air currents, just like the other time. Pretty soon the owl flipped over and down came the eagle with his wings out. He began to soar. And he learned. He learned that he, too, was an eagle.

We heard this some time ago and knew the meaning behind that story. Did you ever have that happen? Sometimes you sit there and your heart is just heavy. It's just heavy and you can't understand how come. Or you feel like you belong somewhere, or there's things people are telling you about yourself and you say, "No, that's not me. I don't think that way."

Except when you write grants and other things, because you have to do those kinds of things in chicken language. We've learned that we have to do that. But we can't forget, we're not chickens. We're eagles.

In this story, the eagles forgot who they were when they lost the guidance of their parents. We, as Indian people, forgot who we were as we lost our world to genocidal wars, epidemic disease, forced dislocations from our lands and the forced loss of our children to Indian boarding schools. Cut off from our history and cultural traditions, a race of sober eagles was defined as drunken chickens. Lies and labels deformed our view of ourselves and our view of Indians as a People. We were taught that our alcohol problems were an expression of our inferiority. We were told that we were alcoholics by birth—that if we drank alcohol, we would inevitably become an alcoholic. We were told that we are born with an insatiable craving for alcohol, that we are hypersensitive to alcohol's effects, and that we are prone to violence when intoxicated. We were told, in short, that a love of alcohol was part of our Indian nature. These "firewater myths" are deadly toxins that have poisoned our minds and shamed our communities for generations.

There is no scientific evidence to support any of these contentions. We are not at risk for alcohol problems because of any racially determined (biological) vulnerability. We are at risk because our personal, family and cultural protective factors have been under sustained assault for hundreds of years. We are at risk because lies have been perpetuated against us that we have believed.

These lies have been heard across so many generations that we have defined alcohol intoxication as an expression of our Indianness—as a personal protest against our attempted colonization. We were taught to poison ourselves and then we were blamed for our own self-destruction. The Wellbriety Movement is asking us to reject these destructive lies. The Wellbriety Movement is asking our intoxicated brothers and sisters, "Why are you acting like a chicken when you are an eagle?" Being drunk is not the Indian way. It is not an effective protest. It is a form of personal and cultural suicide.

It is time Indian People rejected alcohol, not because some Indians develop alcohol problems and alcoholism, but because alcohol is a symbol of efforts to exploit and destroy us as a people. It is time Indian People rejected alcohol because it is not part of our nature. When you return home to your people, spread the truth about our true nature. Tell the people to cast off the lies that have been told about them. Invite them to write a new chapter in our history—a chapter written not with words, but with lives lived in Wellbriety. We will destroy the "Drunken Indian" stereotype with every sober breath we take. We will call upon Indian nations and Indian families to detoxify themselves from the poison that was injected into their histories. We will sweat this poison from our bodies and our minds and rediscover the essence of ourselves as Indian People.

The stereotype of the drunken Indian is the image of the chicken that has been forced upon us. The eagle is the symbol of our sobriety and strength as a people. It is time we declared clearly and boldly: We are not chickens; we are EAGLES! We must teach our children that they are not destined to be chickens, they are destined to be EAGLES! Our new history begins today!

Preface

A lcohol-related problems and alcoholism constitute serious threats to the health and social stability of many Native American and Alaskan Native communities (Indian Health Service, 1995; Westermeyer, 1996), but efforts to forge successful solutions continue to be plagued by "firewater myths" that misrepresent the history, nature, sources and potential solutions to these problems (Leland, 1976). The designation of alcohol as "firewater" within Native history has been attributed to early traders adulterating "Indian Whiskey" with hot peppers and Indians testing the proof of alcohol by seeing if it would burn when thrown into a fire (Abbot, 1996). The term "firewater myths" refers to misconceptions about the source and nature of alcohol problems among Native peoples, the most important of which are that Native people are "constitutionally prone to develop an inordinate craving for liquor and to lose control over their behavior when they drink" (Leland, 1976, p.1).

To portray Native alcohol problems as a biological taint, or to portray alcoholism as the most significant problem facing Native communities, ignores the enormous variability of alcohol problems across and within Native tribes and diverts attention from the political, economic and cultural conditions within which Native alcohol problems first arose and have been sustained (Westermeyer, 1974). To speak of Native alcohol problems without speaking of successful Native prevention and recovery movements constitutes a harmful misrepresentation that has endured for more than two centuries (Trimble, 1988).

There have been recent efforts to accurately reconstruct the historical relationship between Native peoples and alcohol--from the work of MacAndrew and Edgerton (1969) through the recent work of Thatcher (2004). Unfortunately, most of this knowledge lies buried within the scholarly literature while racial stereotypes continue to masquerade as historical facts within the popular culture. Our goal in the coming pages is to weave this recently revealed evidence into a meaningful whole that challenges how the dominant culture has viewed Native American alcohol problems and how Native peoples have viewed their own personal and cultural relationships with alcohol.

In this book, we will offer the historical evidence of how Native peoples resisted and recovered, and today continue to resist and recover, from alcoholism and other alcohol-related problems. The heart of our story unfolds in the mid-eighteenth century, spans the nineteenth and twentieth centuries, and continues with long-enduring and new recovery movements among Native peoples. Twelve "truths" constitute the backbone of this story:

About Native Peoples and Alcohol-Related Problems

1. Native Americans possessed an exceptional knowledge of botanical psychopharmacology prior to European contact. They lived in harmony with the power of these plant-based substances (including alcohol in some tribes) by respecting the spirits and rules of the plants from which they were derived.

2. The initial response of Native tribes to alcohol availability following European contact was not one of drunken mayhem and widespread alcoholism.

3. Alcohol problems and alcoholism rose as Native tribes came under physical and cultural assault and when drinking alcohol shifted from a ritual of intercultural contact to a tool of economic, political and sexual exploitation.

4. Early "firewater myths" portraying Native Americans as genetically inferior (inherently vulnerable to alcoholism) provided ideological support for the decimation and colonization of Native tribes and continue to serve that function today.

5. The legacies of the "firewater myths" include generations of stigma (the "drunken Indian" stereotype), racial shame, and a fundamental misconstruction of the sources of, and solutions to, alcohol problems in Native communities.

6. Native leaders actively resisted the infusion of alcohol into tribal life and continue to resist such infusion today.

About Native Peoples and Alcohol-Related Problems

7. Early indigenous responses to alcohol problems included the development of sobriety-based religious/cultural revitalization and healing movements that constitute the first recovery mutual aid societies in the world--a century before the Washingtonian revival of the 1840s and two centuries before the founding of Alcoholics Anonymous.

8. Recovery traditions in Native communities continue today through abstinence-based spirituality, the "Indianization" of Alcoholics Anonymous and Al-Anon, new recovery-based cultural revitalization movements (e.g., the Wellbriety Movement), and the rise of culturally-informed alcoholism treatment.

9. The most effective and enduring solutions to Native alcohol problems have emerged and continue to emerge from within the very heart of tribal cultures.

10. The history of resistance and recovery within Native American tribes is a testimony to cultural forces of prevention and healing that continue to constitute powerful, but underutilized, antidotes to alcohol problems.

11. A period of great healing, recovery, renewal and resilience has begun within Native communities.

12. Recovery from alcohol problems and alcoholism is a living reality in Native American communities and has been for more than 250 years.

We have provided documentation of the sources that support these conclusions, but we do so with the recognition that traditional scholarly resources often fail to accurately reconstruct early Native American history. Historical documents recorded by non-Natives are particularly problematic. Non-Native observers of Native cultures brought particular biases to their choices of what and what not to record and their own interpretations of what they observed or were told (Stratton, 1981). Many Native stories are missing from written history because Native tribes withheld or selectively interpreted knowledge of their cultures to outsiders out of a fear that such knowledge would be misunderstood or used against them. To counter such omissions and distortions, we have tried to balance the use of archival records with oral histories of tribes that are central to our story. We include such oral histories with the awareness that certain aspects of Native experience are not discussed in any context and as a result will leave voids within parts of the story we are trying to tell. Because so much Native history has been lost, the reader will likely share our wonder about how many Native recovery and revitalization movements not recounted here escaped documentation and are forever lost. That our story is woefully incomplete does not diminish its power as a testimony to Native resistance and recovery.

We have written this book for multiple audiences. For Native people who have not yet found the Red Road, we offer you the gift of your own history--accounts of thousands of Native people who found sobriety, their heritage and their reclaimed selves on the Red Road. For the preventionists and addiction treatment specialists, we offer evidence of the power of revitalized Native culture as a medium of personal, family and community transformation. To policy makers and researchers, we invite you to see Native alcohol and other drug problems in a larger historical and cultural perspective. To tribal leaders, we offer a humble reminder of the power of community, the power of sober leadership and the inseparability of personal and community health.

We have tried to reflect in our language the diversity of how the aboriginal peoples of the Americas refer to themselves. As such we use the terms Native Americans, American Indians, Indian Peoples,

Native Peoples, Indigenous Peoples, Aboriginal Peoples and First Nations Peoples interchangeably in this text. We have also tried to reflect the enormous variation in spelling of names of tribes and individuals by choosing the latest rendition of spelling preferred by a tribe or an individual and then placing alternative spellings in parentheses (the latter to aid readers who wish to pursue further research.)

It is time the "firewater myths" were replaced with the rich history of Native resistance and recovery.

Don Coyhis
Colorado Springs CO
September, 2005

Bill White
Port Charlotte FL
September, 2005

References

Abbot, P.J. (1996). American Indian and Alaska native aboriginal use of alcohol in the United States. *American Indian and Alaskan Native Mental Health Research, 7*:1-13.

Indian Health Service (1995). *Trends in Indian Health, 1995.* Washington, D.C.:DHHS, Public Health Service.

Leland, J. (1976). *Firewater Myths: North American Indian Drinking and Alcohol Addiction,* New Brunswick, New Jersey: Rutgers Center of Alcohol Studies Monograph No. 11.

MacAndrew, C. and Edgerton, R. (1969). *Drunken Comportment.* Chicago: Aldine Publishing Company.

Stratton, R. (1981). Indian alcoholism programs and Native American culture. In: Paredes, A., Ed., *The Alcoholism Services Delivery System.* San Francisco: Jossey-Bass.

Thatcher, R. (2004). *Fighting Firewater Fictions: Moving Beyond the Disease Model of Alcoholism in First Nations.* Toronto: University of Toronto Press.

Trimble. J.E. (1988). Stereotypical images, American Indians and prejudice. In P. Katz and D. Taylor, Eds. *Eliminating Racism: Profiles in Controversy.* New York, Plenum, pp.181-201.

Westermeyer, J. (1996). Alcoholism among New World Peoples: A critique of history, methods, and findings. *American Journal on Addictions, 5*(2),110-123.

Westermeyer, J. (1974). "The drunken Indian:" Myths and realities. *Psychiatric Annals, 4*(11):29-36.

Part One: The Rise of Indian Alcohol Problems

The severe alcohol problems of North American Indians are parallel to those encountered by conquered indigenous peoples throughout the world.

—Gene Thin Elk, Lakota

Wittich Towhartu—Aboriginal Alcohol Awareness:
Save the Slaughter of Our Culture.
Courtesy Adam Bessell/Australia

Chapter One

Before Columbus:
Ritualized and Ceremonial Drug Use

Two million indigenous peoples lived within 600 tribes in the cultural cradle of the Americas before the first European stepped foot on what was clearly not a "new world." In arctic, plains, woodlands, river, coastal and island cultures dating to 50,000 years B.C., Native Peoples spoke more than 500 distinct languages, practiced innumerable religions, and participated in elaborate intertribal trading economies. These cultures contained systems of science and mathematics, highly refined healing practices, spellbinding architecture, orally transmitted histories and myths, and elaborate rituals of daily living. From nomadic hunters to residents of centuries-old settlements, they were (and are today) not one culture but hundreds (Schlesinger, 1993). Columbus called the Native People he encountered *Indios*, in his belief that he had landed in the East Indies. The anglicized version *"Indians"* eventually achieved popular use. The term that preceded it *"Americans"* was applied for several decades to Native peoples, and not to the early colonists (Cherrington, 1926, p. 31). Indigenous peoples had no sense of themselves as a single race of people prior to European contact. Their identities were drawn from connection to family, clan and tribe; it was Europeans who defined them collectively as "Indians" (Kehoe, 1989).

Indigenous peoples of the Americas shared an extremely sophisticated understanding of plant-based medicines. At the time of initial European contact, Old World physicians used less than ten plant-based drugs in their healing practices. At this same time, Native tribes in Americas used more than 170 plant-based medicines (Vogel, 1973), and used methods of drug administration completely unknown in Europe (e.g., smoking, nasal insufflation, rectal injection) (Westermeyer, 1996). Native use of botanical drugs included a wide variety of psychoactive plants, including very potent forms of tobacco and such hallucinogens as sophora, datura, peyote, teonanacatl (psilocybin), ololiuqui (morning glory), mandrake, and fly-agaric (Safford, 1906; Furst, 1976; Westermeyer, 1988, 1991; Rudgley, 1994; Furst, 1986). Native Hawaiians used Kava, an intoxicating alkaloid found in the roots of the plant Piper methysticum (Lurie, 1974).

Two views of datura, also called jimson weed

Before European contact, most Native tribes had no contact with alcohol in any form, and the use of distilled alcohol was limited to tribes in Mexico and the extreme Southwest prior to European contact (Abbot, 1996; Bourke, 1893, 1894). Indigenous tribes in what is today the Southwestern (and possibly the Southeastern) United States, Central America, South America, Caribbean Islands, and Alaska were making and drinking Native forms of beer and wine before European contact. It is possible that contact with alcohol occurred outside the Southwest, but such evidence is scant by comparison. There are some references to the use of palm wine and intoxicating drinks made from berries among Southeastern tribes and brief reports of a beer made from corn by the Hurons in the Northeast, but these may have been consumed before full fermentation. What is clearly lacking are reports of intoxication and drunkenness (Abbott, 1996).

Psilocybin mushrooms (left) and ololiuqui (morning glory, right)

Many Southwestern tribes (e.g., the Pima, Tohono O'Odham/Papago, Apache, Coahulitec, Yuma, and Pueblo) had intoxicating beverages (wine, beer) before European contact and integrated alcohol into ceremonial rituals without harm to individual or tribe. Alcohol was introduced to these tribes from Indian tribes in Mexico who had learned to make more than forty types of alcoholic beverages from such products as honey, corn, plums, cactus, and pineapples (Abbott, 1996). References to two alcoholic drinks made from the maguey (Aloe) plant (pulque, which was a beer-like product made by fermentation, and mescal, a product made by baking and boiling the heart of the plant) suggest some knowledge of distillation (Bourke, 1894; LaBarre, 1938).

It is among the Aztecs that one can glean the potential existence of pre-contact alcohol problems, as suggested by their harsh penalties against intoxication (Cherrington, 1925-1926; Westermeyer and Baker, 1986). But even the Aztec, whose punishments for intoxication ranged from public disgrace to death, controlled alcohol use by prohibiting drinking prior to maturity, limiting quantities of alcohol intake (more than five gourds was prohibited), and ritualizing intoxication within particular ceremonies, e.g., naming, marriage and harvest ceremonies (Vaillant, 1962. pp. 145-146) Within Aztec culture, the "holy nature" of alcohol prevented its secular use as an intoxicating beverage (Paredes, 1975).

Kava (left) from Hawaii, and maquey from Mexico (right)

Native peoples prized altered states of consciousness and ritualized these experiences in ways that contributed to the well-being of their tribes (Loeb, 1943; Levy and Kunitz, 1974). They induced these altered states of perception and experience by fasting, drumming, singing, chanting, dancing, seclusion, exposure to the elements, meditation, sleep-deprivation, physical ordeals, and through the use of botanical drugs. The vision quest, experienced in solitude and in groups, was a central theme in many Native cultures and religions. Visions were a means of spiritual communication--a doorway into the spiritual world and a pathway to enlightenment and healing. The ingestion of the plant was a way of taking the spirit into oneself.

What is most striking about the Native Peoples' relationship with psychoactive drugs before European contact is the marked absence of what today would be called psychoactive drug *abuse* (Abbot, 1996). The potential physical and behavioral toxicity of psychoactive drugs was well understood, and elaborate rituals and taboos guided their use and minimized their untoward effects (Weil, 1972). This was true even in those tribes that had alcohol prior to European contact (Abbot, 1996). These tribes minimized problems with alcohol by one or more of the following strategies:

- rejecting alcohol as a culturally-sanctioned intoxicant,
- reducing exposure of children and (in some tribes) women to alcohol,
- defining intoxication as a sacred state and discouraging the informal, secular use of alcohol,
- defining the right to get intoxicated as a prerogative only of the mature or the elderly,
- limiting the quantities of alcohol that could be consumed,
- limiting the frequency of intoxication (to religious or other ceremonial events such as rites of passage into manhood, marriage, harvest or times of sickness),
- defining alcohol consumption as a component of a ceremony, not its central purpose, and
- ritually structuring the consumption of alcohol in ways that minimized risks (Waddell and Everett, 1979).

An example of the use of cultural controls to minimize alcohol problems and alcoholism can be found among the Pima-Maricopa tribe. The Pima, like a number of Southwestern tribes, limited consumption/intoxication of Native wine to an annual ceremony. Even then, only a third of the tribe indulged at a time with the other two-thirds caring for those who were drinking and assuring the maintenance of order (Bancroft, 1882). This placement of alcohol within the context of religious ritual served as an important protective device. Only the Apache maintained secular consumption of alcohol during this early period--secular defined as use of alcohol outside of the context of ceremony and the lack of any religious attributes attached to the plants from which alcohol was made (Loeb, 1943-44). Another example of cultural controls was the belief that the leadership of the tribe should be held to the highest standards of sobriety because their intoxication posed the greatest threat to the health and safety of the tribe. An example of such a standard can be found among the Seneca in post-contact America, whose first constitution threatened demotion of leaders who consumed alcohol (Abrams, 1976).

In summary, many Native tribes used psychoactive drugs, including alcohol, prior to European contact, but there is no evidence that such use resulted in sustained drunkenness or the clinical condition of alcoholism or addiction. Where used, alcohol and other drugs were highly ritualized in ways that dramatically reduced the risks that intoxicants posed to the individual, family and the tribe. Even after European contact, some Native tribes (e.g., in eastern Washington and northern California) extended such cultural control over alcohol by prescribing it within the sacred rituals of the past. The isolation of these tribes prevented the infusion of more destructive drinking patterns (Thomas, 1981).

Tobacco twist used today for sacred or ceremonial purposes. This tobacco is grown and prepared in a sacred manner and not used addictively in the fashion of commercial tobacco products.

The lesson to be drawn from this earliest era of Native history is that culture and community are the ultimate tools for preventing alcohol and other drug problems. When Native cultures were vibrant, psychoactive plants were viewed as animate and respected. Ceremonial plants such as tobacco, sage, sweetgrass, jimsonweed, and peyote were viewed as containing spirits and were personified through such designations as "Old Man (or Grandfather) Peyote" (Watts, 2001). Each plant, each rock, each person was understood to have a purpose. Any relationship with the plant—and it was viewed as a relationship--occurred within prescribed frameworks that reflected an understanding of that purpose. These frameworks defined virtually every aspect of the drug experience from who could use to when use could occur, from the preparation of the drug to ritual context of its use. Dire consequences could unfold when the spirit was disrespected via breaking its rules. That principle still exists. Consider the experience of one of the authors (Coyhis):

> *I was given the knowledge of a plant--a medicine called Changing Woman--because those who bestowed this gift thought I was spiritually ready for the experience. I learned to hear the voice of the plant, and it brought great meaning to me. But then I misused it. I showed off with it and, as a result, the medicine no longer works. The voice disappeared. When a drug is disrespected, it withdraws its blessings and can wound you.*

Alcohol and other drugs became destructive in Native communities when relationships with them shifted from an I-Thou relationship to an I-It relationship--when they became objects to be used outside the context of sacred ritual. Prevention in this view is about personal and cultural harmony and balance; addiction is a consequence of disharmony (personal and cultural) and excess.

Everything on the planet--animals, plants, everything in our environment--has a set of principles, laws and values under which they function. Everything has an innate knowledge of itself--the bear, the eagle, every plant, each human being. Each of us has an innate knowledge, an internal blueprint, of what it takes for us to live out our destiny as a human being.   We are healthy when we live within that destiny and become sick when we drift from that destiny. Native peoples created their clans and societies to preserve and pass on that knowledge of themselves and how to live in harmony with all things, including plant-based psychoactive drugs.   By all accounts, such harmony did exist before European contact. In the next chapter, we will see how Native peoples initially sustained that harmony when alcohol was first introduced by European explorers and traders.

Three plants used extensively today for ceremonial purposes. Flat cedar (rear), northern plains sage (center), and a braid of sweetgrass looped over the sage, as well as far right.

References

Abbot, P.J. (1996). American Indian and Alaska native aboriginal use of alcohol in the United States. *American Indian and Alaskan Native Mental Health Research,* 7:1-13.

Abrams. G.J. (1976). *The Seneca People.* Phoenix, AZ: Indian Tribal Series.

Bancroft, H. (1882). *The Native Races: Wild Tribes (Volume I)* San Francisco: A.L. Bancroft and Co.

Bourke, J.G. (1893). Primitive distillation among the Tarascoes. *The American Anthropologist,* 6:65-69.

Bourke, J.G. (1894). Distillation by early American Indians. *The American Anthropologist,* 7:297-299.

Cherrington, E. (1925-1926). Ed. *Standard Encyclopedia of the Alcohol Problem,* (Six Volumes). Westerville, Ohio, American Issue Publishing Company.

Furst, P. (1976). *Hallucinogens and Culture.* San Francisco: Chandler & Sharp Publishers, Inc.

Furst, P. (1986). *Mushrooms: Psychedelic Fungi.* London: Burke Publishing Company Limited.

Kehoe, A. (1989). *The Ghost Dance: Ethnohistory and Revitalization.* New York: Holt, Rinehart and Winston.

LaBarre, W. (1938). Native American beers. *American Anthropologist,* 40:224-234.

Levy, J.E. and Kunitz, S.J. (1974). *Indian Drinking: Navajo Practices and Anglo-American Theories,* New York: Wiley.

Loeb, E.M. (1943-1944). Primitive intoxicants. *Quarterly Journal of Studies on Alcohol,* 4:387-398.

Lurie, N. (1974). The world's oldest on-going protest demonstration: North American Indian drinking patterns In: Hundley, N. Ed. *The American Indian.* Santa Barbara, California: CLIO Books, pp.55-76

Paredes. A. (1975). Social control of drinking among the Aztec Indians of Mesoamerica. *Quarterly Journal of Studies on Alcohol,* 36:1139-1153.

Rudgley, R. (1994). *Essential Substances: A Cultural History of Intoxicants.* NY: Kodansha International.

Safford, E. (1906). Narcotic plants and stimulants of the ancient Americans. *Annual Report of the Smithsonian Institution,* pp. 387-429.

Schlesinger, A., Jr. (1993). *The Almanac of American History.* NY: Barnes & Noble.

Thin Elk, G. (1981). Walking in balance on the Red Road. *Journal of Emotional and Behavioral Problems, Fall,* pp. 54-57.

Thomas, R.K. (1981). The history of Native American Indian alcohol use as a community-based phenomenon. In Heath, D.B.; Waddell, J.O.; and Topper, M.D., Eds. *Cultural Factors in Alcohol Research and Treatment of Drinking Problems. Journal of Studies on Alcohol Supplement,* pp.929-39.

Vaillant, G. (1962). *The Aztecs of Mexico.* New York: Doubleday.

Vogel, V. (1970). *American Indian Medicine.* Norman, Oklahoma: University of Oklahoma Press.

Waddell, J.O. and Everett, M.W. (1979). *Drinking behavior among southwestern Indians: An anthropological perspective.* Tucson: University of Arizona Press.

Watts, L. (2001). Applying a cultural models approach to American Indian substance dependency research, *American Indian and Alaska Native Mental Health Research, 10*(1):38-54.

Weil, A. (1972). *The Natural Mind.* Boston: Houghton Mifflin Company.

Westermeyer, J. (1988). The pursuit of intoxication: Our 100 century-old Romance with Psychoactive Substances. *American Journal of Drug and Alcohol Abuse,* 14:175-187.

Westermeyer, J. (1991). Historical and social context of psychoactive substance disorders. In Frances, R. and Miller, S. (eds.). *Clinical Textbook of Addictive Disorders* NY: The Guilford Press.

Westermeyer, J. (1996). Alcoholism among New World Peoples: A critique of history, methods, and findings. *American Journal on Addictions, 5*(2),110-123.

Westermeyer, J. and Baker, J. (1986). Alcoholism and the American Indian. In N.S. Estes and M.E. Heineman (Eds.) *Alcoholism: Development, Consequences, and Interventions.* 3rd edition, pp. 273-282. St. Louis: Mosby.

Chapter Two

Initial Post-contact Drinking Patterns

No single description or explanation can fully depict the relationship between Native peoples and alcohol during the extended period (from the fifteenth to mid-nineteenth century) of first European contact. These first contacts with Native tribes came from the Spanish in the South, from the English, French, Dutch, and Swedish in the East, and from the Russians in the Northwest and Alaska. Native relationships with alcohol varied by invading groups and tribes, varied by geographical area, and varied over the extended period of Euro-Indian contact. However, two points are clear: 1) the near-universal presence of alcohol in all initial contacts between non-Native and Native peoples (Cherrington, 1920; Jilek-Aall, 1981), and 2) the fact that the initial Native response to alcohol exposure was not one of instant devastation (Heath, 1983). The historical studies of MacAndrew and Edgerton (1969), Mancall (1995), Unrau (1996), Dempsey (2002) and the analysis of Frank, Moore, and Ames (2000) all provide evidence that early Native responses to alcohol changed from a benign pattern of harmless drinking to a destructive pattern of high-dose binge drinking only after Native tribes came under increasing physical and cultural assault.

The history of American Indian and Alaskan Native responses to post-Columbian alcohol exposure is often painted as one of drunken mayhem and alcoholism. The reality is much more complex and nuanced than the myth. There was great variation in how different Native individuals and different tribes responded to alcohol. Reports from Jacques Cartier to Lewis and Clark document that many Native Peoples either did not drink alcohol or drank in moderation. For example, when Lewis and Clark made initial contact with the Assiniboine tribe in 1804, they recorded the following response to their offering of alcohol as a gift: "They [the Assiniboine] say we are no friend or we would not give them what makes them fools" (Lewis and Clark, 1904, p. 199). A 1789 description of the early introduction of alcohol in trading with the Blackfoot noted that the Blackfoot were not "enervated by the use of spirituous liquors," that they "drink moderately" and are not "slaves to it" (Quoted in Dempsey, 2002, p.7). The story in the Northwest and Alaska is a quite similar one. When alcohol was first introduced to Native tribes by the Russians in 1741, their response was generally one of "distaste and suspicion." The very first response of a Native Alaskan to alcohol offered as a gift from the Russians produced the following response: he "spat the gin out at once and turning to his fellows screeched most horribly" (quoted in Fortuine, 1992, p. 279). The Tlingit, Tsimpsian and Haida tribes viewed alcohol as a tool of trickery that would render then vulnerable to attack and put them in the "power of the Russians" (Lemert, 1954, p. 305). During the earliest introduction of distilled alcohol into Alaska, alcohol was a much greater problem for the Russians than for Alaskan Natives (Fortuine, 1992).

Craig MacAndrew and Robert Edgerton reviewed the early Native encounters with alcohol in their classic study, *Drunken Comportment*. They concluded that, in the historical relationship between alcohol and Native Peoples, "the early days were the good old days." They note that many Native Peoples loathed alcohol and considered it unnatural to drink anything so disgusting to the senses.

Some tribes condemned liquor as a poison and saw drunkenness as "degrading to free men" (Andersen, 1988). Native leaders called alcohol the "waters of death." Frederikson (1932), in his review of early tribal responses to alcohol, noted the presence of tribes that rejected alcohol in spite of sustained attempts to institute the whiskey traffic among them. Even where alcohol problems arose, these were not universal within a tribe. Scomp, in his description of the rise of alcohol problems among Native tribes in Georgia, noted: "there are many sober men among them who abhor the use of liquor" (Scomp, 1988, p. 55).

Most Native people who did drink alcohol showed "remarkable restraint while in their cups." Many drank alcohol, but only during the infrequent contact with white traders. Intoxication under such circumstances did not reflect their normal daily life and habits. Others drank and learned to seek out the experience of intoxication. Even in this group, different people responded differently to intoxication. Some sang or became quiet and meditative, while others imitated the wild, violent, and morally compromised states of intoxication modeled by traders. Although isolated accounts of destructive drinking by Native peoples can be found in this early contact period, most drank in socially acceptable ways or didn't drink at all (MacAndrew and Edgerton, 1969; Mancall, 1995; Mosher, 1975; Phillips, 1961).

Many Native tribes incorporated alcohol into their cultures as a result of their contact with the Euro-American traders. The new practice of drinking fermented and distilled alcohol was begun by Native tribes. Native Americans used alcohol:

- to express friendship and generosity, sexual attraction, and courage
- to experience and express physical and spiritual power
- within mourning ceremonies,
- within healing rituals, particularly to relieve pain, and

- for exchange among tribes as a means of strengthening intertribal alliances (Mancall, 1995; Hill, 1990).

As a new intoxicant, alcohol masked its long-term devastation behind short-term effects that often enhanced traditional Native values. Even where alcohol was embraced, it was embraced with ambivalence. The roots of such ambivalence are reflected in the Lakota name for alcohol, *mni wakan*, which has a dual meaning: "magic water" and "the water that makes men foolish" (Bordewich, 1996, p. 256).

A 1599 artwork depicts indigenous peoples of Guiana in northeastern South America drinking alcohol. The caption accompanying this photo in Mancall, 1995, p. 65 quotes the original Latin caption to the painting, stating, "The people of the kingdom of Guiana…are completely given over to drunkenness and surpass all nations in drinking." The drawing is done in a distinctively European Renaissance style of the day. Courtesy, The Historical Society of Pennsylvania.

Distilled alcohol and the way it was used by Europeans marked a break in the way Native tribes had related to plant-based psychoactive drugs. What Europeans introduced was not just a new psychoactive drug, but the use of drugs in a secularized (non-religious, non-medicinal), domesticated (daily beverage) and recreational (solely for pleasure) manner. European attitudes killed the spirits in the plants and turned the plants into "things." What was once a relationship of respect between the person and the plant spirit became the exploitation of a spiritless object. Native knowledge, beliefs and rituals had protected Native people from the potentially harmful effects of psychoactive drugs. We will see in the next chapter how, as Native cultures came under European assault, the cultural armor of protection weakened.

References

Anderson, T.I. (1988). *Alaska Hooch.* Fairbanks, AK: Hoo-Che-Noo.

Bordewich, F. (1996). *Killing the White Man's Indian.* New York: Anchor Books.

Cherrington, E. (1920). *The Evolution of Prohibition in the United States.* Westerville, Ohio: The American Issue Press.

Dempsey, H. (2002). *Firewater: The Impact of the Whiskey Trade on the Blackfoot Nation.* Calgary: Fifth House Ltd.

Fortuine, R. (1992). *Chills and Fever: Health and Disease in the Early History of Alaska.* Fairbanks: University of Alaska Press.

Frank, J.W., Moore, R.S. & Ames, G.M. (2000). Historical and cultural roots of drinking problems among American Indians. *American Journal of Public Health,* 90(3), 344-51.

Frederikson, O. (1932). *The Liquor Question Among the Indian Tribes in Kansas: 1804-1881.* Lawrence, Kansas: University of Kansas.

Heath, D. (1983). Alcohol use among North American Indians: A cross-cultural survey of patterns and problems. In: *Research Advances in Alcohol and Drug Problems, Volume 7,* Ed. By Reginald Smart, et.al., NY: Plenum Press, pp. 343-396.

Hill, T.W. (1990). Peyotism and the control of heavy drinking: The Nebraska Winnebego in the early 1900's. *Human Organization, 49*(3).255-265.

Jilek-Aall, L. (1981). Anomic depression, alcoholism and a culture-congenial Indian response. *Journal of Studies on Alcohol,* Supplement No. 9, 159-170.

Lemert, E. (1954). *Alcohol and the Northwest Coast Indians.* Berkeley: University of California Press.

Lewis, M and Clark, W. (1904). *The Original Journals of the Lewis and Clark Expedition 1804-1806.* Ed. by R.G. Thwaites, New York: Dodd Mead & Company.

MacAndrew, C. and Edgerton, R. (1969). *Drunken Comportment.* Chicago: Aldine Publishing Company.

Mancall, P. (1995). *Deadly Medicine: Indians and Alcohol in Early America.* Ithaca, NY: Cornell University Press.

Mosher, J. (1975). *Liquor Legislation and Native Americans: History and Perspective.* Working Paper F 136. Berkely: Social Research Group, University of California.

Philips, P. (1961). *The Fur Trade.* Norman: University of Oklahoma.

Scomp, H.A. (1888). *King Alcohol in the Realm of King Cotton.* Chicago, IL: Blakley.

Unrau, William (1996). *White Man's Wicked Water: The Alcohol Trade and Prohibition in Indian Country, 1802-1892.* Lawrence: University Press of Kansas.

Chapter Three

The Rise of Native Alcohol Problems

*The severe alcohol problems of North American Indians are
parallel to those encountered by conquered indigenous
peoples throughout the world.*

—Gene Thin Elk

There are three themes that emerge in historical accounts of the rise of alcohol related problems among Native tribes during the eighteenth and nineteenth centuries: 1) the growing use of alcohol as a tool in the political, economic, and sexual exploitation of Native peoples, 2) the pattern of violent, binge drinking of frontier Euro-American people as a model for Native drinking, and 3) the rise of alcohol problems in tandem with Native population decimation (via wars, epidemics of contagious disease, starvation), the loss of ancestral lands, forced relocation, poverty and utter demoralization (Hawkins and Blume, 2002).

Disputes over treaties and the loss of Native lands can often be traced to the role that alcohol played as a tool of political manipulation. There is little doubt that alcohol served as a weapon of manipulation in the acquisition of Native lands and the displacement of Native peoples. Studies of Indian trading practices note how traders would promote alcohol dependence and then trade whiskey for mortgages on Native land (Gonzalez, 1977). Jacobs (1950) reports on a great Indian conference held in the June of 1755 at which the white negotiators brought six kegs of rum into the council rooms of the great conference. He describes the exploitive use of alcohol in Indian diplomacy as follows:

> *...interpreters deliberately used the Indian's fascination for liquor to dupe him into selling his lands in exchange for cheap presents. There were a few chiefs who were able to 'hold' their liquor day after day and still transact business, much to the amazement of their tormentors.* (Jacobs, 1950, pp, 53-53)

Some historical accounts have also identified the traffic and consumption of alcohol as a major factor in the Indian Wars (Furnas, 1965).

Alcohol use during business or treaty events amounted to alcohol's use as a weapon o manipulation against Native Peoples. "Treaty Makers." Unknown artist, c. 1840 Courtesy, National Museum of the American Indian Smithsonian Institution, New York.

Alcohol was used as a tool of pacification during this period. Spanish officials in the Southwest encouraged drinking among those tribes most prone to violently resist European incursion. The goal was to control these tribes by making them dependent upon the Spanish for supplies of distilled spirits (Levy and Kunitz, 1974). There were also times that alcohol served as a weapon of war. For example, Jacobs (1950, p. 59) describes an incident in 1684/85 in which a "Mr. De la Salle, having regaled the People [Native Americans] and made them Drunk, while he kept his own sober, afterwards put them all to Death." In 1774, white frontiersmen invited a group of Shawnee Indians to their encampment, plied them with liquor until they were intoxicated and then murdered them (Edmunds, 1983). Similar reports of inducement to intoxication and massacre continued into the late 1800s (Kennedy, 1997).

Alcohol was an essential element of the fur trade in regions where fur-bearing animals were plentiful and encouragement of Native drinking grew as competition between trading companies intensified (Hamer and Steinbring, 1980). A central trading strategy was to cultivate Native people's dependence on alcohol and then to supply it in great quantities and at greater frequencies than could one's competitors (Dempsey, 2002). During the late 1700s and early 1800s, deceitful traders made a regular practice of encouraging intoxication among Native peoples, hoping to get Native goods at the lowest possible prices. Trading would often not begin until the Native representatives were intoxicated. To maximize their trading advantage, White traders prepared special blends of drugged and doctored alcohol known generically as "Indian Whiskey." Lender and Martin (1982) described one such recipe as follows: 1 gallon of Missouri River water, 2 gallons of alcohol, 2 ounces of strychnine, 3 plugs of tobacco, 5 bars of soap, 2 pound of red pepper, and an unspecified quantity of sagebrush. Other common ingredients included burnt sugar, red ink, Jamaica Ginger, sulfuric acid, gunpowder, turpentine, nitric acid, camphor, cologne, vanilla extract, tea, and tincture of opium (Andersen, 1988; Lemert, 1954; Kennedy, 1997; Dempsey, 2002). When Indian Whiskey began crossing the border as a trade item with Indian tribes in Canada, an 1859 regulation was passed that prohibited the adulteration of alcohol with such toxic substances as vitriol, turpentine and strychnine (Dempsey, 2002).

Traders would arrive in Native villages with 30 or 40 kegs of adulterated whiskey and take a season's worth of skins for their watered-down booze. Two common and particularly exploitive strategies were exorbitant pricing and selling Native Americans alcohol on credit (Mancall, 1995; Unrau, 1996). For example, whiskey selling for $1 a gallon elsewhere sold for $30 a gallon in Indian Country. When Kunitz and Levy (1994) reviewed the role of alcohol in nineteenth century trading practices in the Southwest, they concluded that the economies of many non-Indian communities were dependent upon cultivating Native dependence upon alcohol. In Alaska, such dependence was cultivated by the Russians by using rum as the primary payment for seal fur and by attempting to prohibit the Aleuts from making their own alcohol (Prinz, 1995).

Trading of alcohol to Natives was widely banned, but enforcement was sporadic to non-existent. Laws banning the Indian alcohol trade were frequently ignored or repealed (Mosher, 1975). Even where offenders were apprehended, they often escaped conviction due to the intimidation of Indian witnesses and the manipulations of legal counsel provided by the wealthy men by whom the traders were often employed (Kennedy, 1997). Even when convicted, penalties could be as little as a day in jail and a $25 fine--a minor inconvenience considered the enormous profits involved (McNitt, 1962). Another little known role alcohol played in the exploitation of Native people involved its role in the Indian slave trade. This trade involved getting Native people intoxicated, provoking them into some act of outrage and then arresting and sentencing them to servitude. Such punishment usually meant being sold into slavery and transported to the West Indies--a practice that further depleted many tribes (Cherrington, 1925-26).

Because of the trading patterns, Native villages spent much of their time with no available alcohol, then suddenly came into contact with huge quantities of alcohol. This shaped a pattern of communal, socially destructive binge drinking that for many tribes was modeled on the "frontier drinking" patterns of the explorers, trappers, traders, soldiers, cowboys, prospectors, railroad construction gangs, fishing crews, loggers, and land speculators (Winkler, 1968; Frank, et al, 2000). Native peoples' first experiences with alcohol were modeled on the drinking patterns of white men who were social outcasts from established communities and viewed even by their peers as "desperadoes," "cut-throats" and the "scum of the earth" (Gonzalez, 1977; Kennedy, 1997).

There are many early reports of this pattern of Indian drinking as a learned behavior. Typical of such reports is the following from 1771:

> *...the white people have taught them how to drink the fiery water...The Indians imitate them in it...* (Bossu, 1771, p. 120).

An 1869 report by Vincent Colyer described the type of drinking modeled to Native Alaskans:

> *...examples of drunkenness are set before the Indians almost daily, so that in fact the principal teaching that they are at present receiving is that drunkenness and debauchery are held by us...as indications of our advanced and superior civilization"* (Quoted in Fortuine, 1992, p. 286).

The practice of gulping alcohol (to avoid its confiscation) was further ingrained following federal prohibition of the sale of alcohol to Native people in 1832 (Westermeyer and Baker, 1986). Westermeyer has described how the new drinking rituals introduced into Native tribes differed from pre-contact drug using rituals.

> *This mode of drinking was secular, dependent upon individual rather than group decision, male-centered rather*

than family-oriented and often associated with bravado or confrontation (Westermeyer, 1996, p. 111).

This depiction is further confirmed by Maria Chona's description of the introduction of whiskey to the Tohono O'Odham (Papago) Indians.

> *There were white men here and there on our land at that time, as there never had been. So our men began to learn to drink that whiskey. It was not a thing that you must drink only once a year like our cactus cider. You could drink it any time, with no singing and no speeches, and it did not bring rain. Men grew crazy when they drank that whiskey and had visions* (quoted in Apess, 1833, p. 371).

The evidence that this pattern of communal binge drinking was a learned behavior is reinforced by the fact that more varied patterns of drinking later emerged as Native tribes were exposed to different styles of alcohol consumption (Kunitz and Levy, 1994). The initial pattern of binge drinking that became known as "Indian drinking" is a misnomer. It was and is not uniquely Indian, but a pattern more aptly described in the alcoholism literature as "frontier drinking" or "bottle gang drinking"--a pattern of drinking that has long crossed racial and cultural boundaries (Westermeyer, 1996). What may have institutionalized this pattern of drinking in Native America and prevented the assimilation of White, middle-class drinking patterns was the more than century-long legal prohibition of alcohol in Indian Country (Kelso and DuBay, 1989).

Alcohol also played a role in the sexual exploitation and violence against Native women by traders and soldiers (Andersen, 1988). While sexual relationships between white men and Native women were not uncommon, Native leaders objected to the way in which alcohol was used to induce these relationships. Alcohol-related sexual violence and sexual exploitation of Native women weakened

Native family structure and contributed to the genetic and cultural dilution of Native tribes (Heizer, 1974).

Native tribes were vulnerable to exploitation in part because of their beliefs and values. The use of alcohol was incorporated into rituals that expressed much that was valued in Native tribes: friendship, camaraderie, generosity, hospitality, courage, sexuality and spirituality (Hill, 1990). The ever-present values of hospitality and generosity made many tribes vulnerable to predatory traders. The fact that Native People had no concept of land ownership made them particularly vulnerable to predatory politicians.

Edmund Carpenter (1959) has argued that for tribes such as the Iroquois, alcohol intoxication was an extension of the vision quest tradition, and that Natives valued alcohol for its ability to facilitate mystical experiences.

> *...to the Iroquois, intoxication originally meant not flight, but search; not escape, but fulfillment; not loss of self; but discovery of self* (Carpenter, 1959, p. 150).

Carpenter further contends that the purpose of Native drinking changed over time to one of emotional release and escape. As Native tribes suffered deprivation, demoralization and cultural dissipation, all that was known and valued disappeared. In this context, alcohol intoxication offered a respite from pain and a fleeting experience of power and control over one's destiny (Mancall, 1995). Constantine Scollen, a missionary working with the Blackfoot, described how drinking changed after a devastating and demoralizing smallpox epidemic in 1870.

> *They sold their robes and horses by the hundreds for it [alcohol]....It was painful to see the state of poverty to which they had been reduced. Formerly they had been the most opulent Indians in the country, and now were clothed in rags, without horses and without guns* (Quoted in Dempsey, 2002, p. 136).

Possession of alcohol also became linked to power and status, at a time other sources of power and prestige diminished with the loss of war parties, hunting, and cultural ceremonies (Hamer and Steinbring, 1980). Giving alcohol became integrated into such existing cultural rituals as the potlatch--the gift-giving feast associated with many of the Northwestern tribes (Lemert, 1958).

The pattern of Native drinking that developed over time was one of group-oriented, high-dose binge drinking. In such a context, it should not be surprising that alcoholism took its place alongside cholera, measles, smallpox, yellow fever, malaria, diphtheria, pneumonia, influenza, tuberculosis, and typhoid in wounding Native peoples and their cultures. Alcohol and infectious agents were both purposefully used to "clear the land." For example, blankets known to be infected with smallpox were given to the Delaware Indians in the 1760s by the British from Fort Pitt (Calloway, 1994). What is most amazing in light of this assault is not the number of Native people who died, but the number who survived. The history of this era is as much the story of cultural survival and resilience as it is a story of cultural assault.

But it was not survival without a cost. European invaders wounded Native peoples and offered a balm to salve those wounds--a balm that masked its long-term devastation with a transient amelioration of pain and an equally fleeting experience of power. The balm turned out to be a poison whose only antidote was itself: the painful aftermath of drinking and the renewed sense of loss of culture and loss of self could be relieved only by drinking more alcohol. This set in motion what Prinz has called a "circle of destruction"--the bundling of alcohol intoxication and alcoholism with violence against self, violence against one's own family, and injury to one's own tribe and its culture (Prinz, 1995). Gene Thin Elk (1981) suggests that the infusion of alcohol and other drugs into Native Tribal life desecrated Native cultures and prepared future generations to "pursue escapist, hedonistic, or exploitive lifestyles" and to fill lives marked by "cultural emptiness."

References

Anderson, T.I. (1988). *Alaska Hooch.* Fairbanks, AK: Hoo-Che-Noo.

Apes, W. (1829). *A Son of the Forest. The Experience of William Apes, A Native of the Forest, Comprising a Notice of the Pequod Tribe of Indians, Written by Himself.* New York: By the Author.

Bossu, J. (1771). *Travels through that part of North America formerly called Louisiana* trans. John Reinhold Forster, 2 vols. London, pp. 117-123.

Calloway, C., Ed. (1994). *The World Turned Upside Down: Indian Voices from Early America.* Boston: Bedford Books.

Carpenter, E.S. (1959). Alcohol in the Iroquois dream quest. *American Journal of Psychiatry, 116*:148-151.

Cherrington, E. (1925-1926). Ed. *Standard Encyclopedia of the Alcohol Problem,* (Six Volumes). Westerville, Ohio, American Issue Publishing Company.

Dempsey, H. (2002). *Firewater: The Impact of the Whiskey Trade on the Blackfoot Nation.* Calgary: Fifth House Ltd.

Edmunds, R.D. (1983). *The Shawnee Prophet.* Lincoln: University of Nebraska Press.

Fortuine, R. (1992). *Chills and Fever: Health and Disease in the Early History of Alaska.* Fairbanks: University of Alaska Press.

Frank, J.W., Moore, R.S. & Ames, G.M. (2000). Historical and cultural roots of drinking problems among American Indians. *American Journal of Public Health,* 90(3), 344-51.

Furnas, J. (1965). *The Life and Times of the Late Demon Rum.* London: W.H. Allen.

Gonzalez, M. (1977). Regulation of Indian traders: A historical perspective. *American Indian Law Review, 5*(2):313-342.

Hamer, J. and Steinbring, J. Eds. (1980). *Alcohol and Native Peoples of the North.* Washington, D.C.: University Press of America.

Hawkins, H.H. and Blume, A.W. (2002). Lost of sacredness: Historical context of health policies for Indigenous People in the United States.

In Mail, P. Herutin-Roberts, S, Martcin, S., and Howard, J. Eds. *Alcohol Use Among American Indians and Alaskan Natives* (NIAAA Research Monograph No. 37). Bethesda, MD: National Institute in Alcohol Abuse and Alcoholism, pp. 25-46.

Heizer, R. (1974). *The Destruction of California Indians.* Lincoln, Nebraska: University of Nebraska Press.

Hill, T.W. (1990). Peyotism and the control of heavy drinking: The Nebraska Winnebego in the early 1900's. *Human Organization, 49*(3):255-265.

Jacobs, W.R. (1950). *Diplomacy and Indian Gifts.* Stanford, CA: Stanford University Press.

Kelso, D. and DuBay, W. (1989). *Alaskan Natives and alcohol: A sociological and epidemiological review.* NIAAA Res. Mongr. Series 18:223-238.

Kennedy, M.A. (1997). *The Whiskey Trade of the Northwestern Plains: A Multidisciplinary Study.* New York: Peter Lang.

Kunitz, S. and Levy, J. (1994). *Drinking Careers: A Twenty-five Year Study of Three Navaho Populations.* New Haven, CT: Yale University Press.

Lemert, E. (1954). *Alcohol and the Northwest Coast Indians.* Berkeley: University of California Press.

Lemert, E. (1958). The use of alcohol in three Salish Indian Tribes. *Quarterly Journal of Studies on Alcohol, 29*:90-107.

Lender, M and Martin, J. (1982). *Drinking in America.* NY: The Free Press.

Levy, J.E. and Kunitz, S.J. (1974). *Indian Drinking: Navajo Practices and Anglo-American Theories,* New York: Wiley.

Mancall, P. (1995). *Deadly Medicine: Indians and Alcohol in Early America.* Ithaca, NY: Cornell University Press.

McNitt (1962). *The Indian Traders.* Norman: University of Oklahoma Press.

Mosher, J. (1975). *Liquor Legislation and Native Americans: History and Perspective.* Working Paper F 136. Berkeley: Social Research Group, University of California.

Thin Elk, G. (1981). Walking in balance on the Red Road. *Journal of Emotional and Behavioral Problems Fall,* pp. 54-57.

Prinz, S. (1995). *Contributing Factors and Issues Related to Substance Abuse Among Alaska Natives.* Presented at the Alcohol-Related Problems in Alaska Conference, August 30-September 1.

Unrau, William (1996). *White Man's Wicked Water: The Alcohol Trade and Prohibition in Indian Country, 1802-1892.* Lawrence: University Press of Kansas.

Westermeyer, J. and Baker, J. (1986). Alcoholism and the American Indian. In N.S. Estes and M.E. Heineman (Eds.) *Alcoholism: Development, Consequences, and Interventions.* 3rd edition, pp. 273-282. St. Louis: Mosby.

Westermeyer, J. (1996). Alcoholism among New World Peoples: A critique of history, methods, and findings. *American Journal on Addictions, 5*(2),110-123.

Winkler, A.M. (1968). Drinking on the American frontier. *Quarterly Journal of Studies on Alcohol,* 29: 413-445.

Chapter Four

"Firewater Myths":

Ideas as Weapons of Colonization

In the first three chapters we have described the lack of alcohol and other drug-related problems within American Indian and Alaskan Native tribes prior to European contact, the lack of significant alcohol problems during the earliest period of Euro-Indian contacts, and the rise of Native alcohol problems during an era marked by Euro-Indian conflict and the dislocation, disruption, and demoralization of Native tribal life. The lesson from this history is that individuals and whole groups are vulnerable to alcohol and other drug-related problems during periods of political and cultural colonization. Alcohol problems flourished where Native religious and cultural institutions were weakest and where tribal leaders had been killed, imprisoned or discredited. The destruction of cultural traditions, genetic pollution, and forced geographical migrations all contributed to Native peoples' rising risk for alcohol problems (Westermeyer, 1988).

In this chapter, we will describe the birth of "firewater myths" that defined the source of Native alcohol problems in ways that furthered European designs for the colonization of Native cultures and lands, and that defined for generations how Native Peoples viewed their own relationship to alcohol.

The Firewater Myths

As conflict between Europeans and Native tribes increased, European observations of Native drinking also changed. What were formerly perceived as the intoxication-induced misdeeds of particular individuals were now given a broader racial interpretation. Differences between Native drinking and Anglo-American drinking were noted, exaggerated (or fabricated) and then re-framed in terms of racial superiority and inferiority. White drunkenness was interpreted as the misbehavior of an individual; Native drunkenness was interpreted in terms of the inferiority of a race (Mosher, 1975). This idea of inferiority/superiority can be found as far back as European Contact. What emerged regarding intoxication were four inter-related beliefs about Native Americans and alcohol (Westermeyer, 1974; Schaefer, 1981).

Myth 1.   American Indians have an inborn, insatiable appetite for alcohol.

Views of Native American drinking patterns emerged within a larger conceptualization of Native peoples as "savages," "infidels," "barbarians," and "heathens" (Berkhorer, 1978, p. 15). The caricature of alcohol problems among Native Americans was used to buttress the view that Native people were biologically and culturally inferior to Euro-Americans. Alcohol consumption and intoxication by Euro-Americans was viewed as a prerogative whose excesses were seen as a reflection of personal immoral or (later) medical vulnerability. Native American drinking and intoxication were viewed as a threat to community order and framed in terms of racial pathology (biological and cultural inferiority).

Myth 2. American Indians are hypersensitive to alcohol (cannot "hold their liquor") and are inordinately vulnerable to addiction to alcohol.

In this view, Native people a) lacked the biological capacity to develop tolerance to alcohol, b) became extremely intoxicated on small amounts of alcohol, and c) rapidly developed a physical and psychological addiction to alcohol. The emerging notion that Native drunkenness rested on an inborn biological trait marks the very beginning of the American concept of "addiction" (Mancall, 1997).

Myth 3. American Indians are dangerously violent when intoxicated.

An extension of myth two was the proposition that alcohol released the violence that was thought to be an ingrained element of the Indian temperament. Colonizing groups often project their own actual violence onto the alleged character of those they are colonizing. In American history, such projection is evident in Euro-American fear of violence by Native Americans and African Americans--a fear that generated responses ranging from bounties for Indian scalps to the Slave Codes.

During the eighteenth and nineteenth centuries, these three inter-related myths became part of the larger construction of the image of "Indian" within the Euro-American consciousness. These myths were incorporated into the very fabric of governmental intervention with Native tribes. Consider the following language from an 1897 Minnesota Supreme Court decision:

> *It* [alcohol control statute] *was enacted in view of the well-known social conditions, habits, and tendencies of Indians as a race...it is a well-known fact that Indians as a race are not as highly civilized as the whites; that they are less subject to moral restraint, more liable to acquire an inordinate appetite for intoxicating liquors, and also more liable to be dangerous to themselves and others when intoxicated* (Quoted in Mosher, 1975, p. 29).

William Macleod's 1928, text, *The American Indian Frontier*, further illustrates the perpetuation of the firewater myths. Macleod claimed that Native Americans developed an instantaneous and insatiable craving for alcohol upon first exposure to it, were particularly prone to violence under its effects, and, though recognizing its evil, were "powerless" to check their desire for it (Macleod, 1928, p. 3).

Myth 4.   The solutions to alcohol problems in Native communities lie in resources outside these communities.

This final myth declared that Native Peoples were individually and collectively incapable of resolving alcohol problems without outside intervention. In this view, the solution to alcohol problems was to be found in the abandonment of Native traditions and the embrace of the dominant culture and its social, religious, and medical folkways. This proposition justified the treatment of Native People as dependent wards (recalcitrant children) who required the civilizing influence of a strict parent (the federal government). Thatcher (2004, p. 139) notes the curious assumption in this view that "a group's oppressor can also be relied upon to be its liberator."

The firewater myths served many functions. They reinforced patterns of domination and subjugation at a time of increasing conflict between the indigenous tribes of the Americas and Euro-Americans. They provided embellished tales of violent debauchery among "New World Savages"—tales that were in great demand among European audiences. The myths provided a rationale and scapegoat for the failure of missionaries to Christianize Native Peoples (Dailey, 1979). They also provided diversion for white culpability for the quantity and price of liquor in Indian country and the system of credits and loans that left many Natives hopelessly impoverished.

The four firewater myths summarized here have long-outlived the conditions in which they arose and yet they continue to shape how Native Americans are perceived by others and how we perceive ourselves.

Firewater Myths and Modern Science

While the "firewater myths" were well-timed for their moral, economic and political utility, they are not supported by either the historical or medical/scientific evidence.

Fact One: The history of the rise of alcohol problems in Native communities was reconstructed and perpetuated in conformity with the firewater mythology.

There is a popular conception that the European introduction of alcohol created instant devastation to Native tribes via drunkenness and alcoholism.   This view fails to acknowledge patterns of abstinence and moderate drinking during early Euro-Indian contact and ignores the cultural context in which Native alcohol problems slowly and subsequently developed.   The first three chapters of this book stand as a clear refutation of this view.

Fact Two: The extent and nature of alcohol problems in Native communities continues to be distorted and misrepresented by the failure to use unduplicated counts in epidemiological studies and by framing all Native alcohol problems within the conceptual rubric of alcoholism.

Such practices stigmatize whole tribes and Native Peoples as a whole for the intractable problems of small subcultures of problem drinkers (May, 1994).   Alcohol-related problems are serious public health problems in many Native communities, but the latest and best scientific studies confirm that substance-related problems are not as severe or as pervasive as often portrayed in the professional and popular literature (Spicer, Beals, Croy, Mitchell, Novins, Moore, and Manson, 2003; See also Mitchell, Beals, Novins and Spicer, 2003).

The danger in exaggerating the impact of Native alcohol problems and their impact on individuals and communities is that one then sees alcoholism treatment and alcoholism recovery as panaceas for these individuals and their tribes, when in fact these problems are nested within a much more complex network of political economic and social problems that are linked to the history of Native tribes within the United States (Westermeyer, 1974). It is this nexus between the individual, the community and history that has given the religious and cultural revitalization movements we will later describe such an important role in the resolution of Native alcohol problems.

Womack (1996) has documented the way in which the story of alcohol-related problems in Native communities is told from a perspective that is pathology oriented. Whether a community's cup is portrayed as half full or half empty affects how those in that community perceive themselves individually and collectively and how they relate to the outside world. All too often, Native communities are portrayed with an almost exclusive focus on their problems and deficits. Using the voices of non-Indians to tell the story of Native communities through the lens of pathology (alcoholism) without acknowledging Native strength and resilience (the presence and power of sobriety, recovery and health) misrepresents reality and further wounds these communities. To speak of Native alcoholism and other drug dependencies while remaining silent about Native resistance, resilience and recovery is to lie by omission.

Many of the alcohol-related problems experienced within Native tribes could more technically be described as "alcohol abuse and misuse" (binge drinking combined with high risk behaviors and environments) as opposed to alcoholism (May, 1994). Many Native communities do not suffer from alcoholism as traditionally defined. Berreman, for example, in his review of drinking patterns among the Aleuts, noted that occasional heavy drinking was the norm and that while instances of blackouts, extended sprees, delirium tremens were noted, "no individual repeatedly and continually displayed these symptoms, and all could suspend drinking without adverse consequences" (Berreman, 1956, P. 511). Berreman concluded that alcohol problems among the Aleuts were symptomatic of social disorganization and not the self-contained clinical entity noted in the alcoholism literature.

Native people exhibit quite different drinking patterns and sometimes quite different drinking patterns over the course of their individual lives, from "Indian drinking" (episodic and group-oriented binge drinking), to "white drinking" (time- and dose-limited alcohol use without overt signs of intoxication) to abstinence (Westermeyer, 1974; Lemert, 1982; Weibel-Orlando, 1986-1987). A recent survey of two American Indian populations revealed abstinence rates in older populations ranging from 53% to 63% (Spicer, Beals, Croy, et al, 2003).

Alcohol consumption and the prevalence, pattern and severity of alcohol problems and alcoholism vary widely within and across tribes--even tribes that share geographical proximity (May, 1989; Abbot, 1998). It is as inappropriate to project the alcohol problem rate of the most disrupted Native communities on all Native Peoples as it would be to project the alcoholism rates from predominantly white skid row areas onto all Caucasians (May, 1994).

Fact Three: There has yet to be definitive evidence that Native Peoples physically respond to alcohol differently than other races or possess a unique biological vulnerability to alcoholism (May, 1977; Schafer, 1981; Westermeyer and Baker, 1986; May, 1994; Mancall, 1995; French 2000; Long, et al, 2002).

Recent studies have not confirmed the theory that alcoholism among Native Americans is caused by a biological hypersensitivity to alcohol. One of the most recent of these studies concludes:

> *...the results from the present study do not support the idea that Native Americans are more sensitive to the effects of alcohol...the findings suggest that theories other than the firewater myth are needed to explain patterns of problem drinking among Native Americans.* (Garcia-Andrade, Wall, and Ehlers, 1997).

No gene has been identified that makes Native Americans more susceptible to alcoholism than other races (Schaefer, 1981; Mancall, 1995; Mancall, 1997).   Differences of alcohol metabolism and genetic vulnerability to alcoholism are traits of individuals and families, not traits of racial and ethnic groups (Long, et al, 2002; May, 1994).   There are as many differences in vulnerability to alcohol problems (and the choice to drink or not drink, the frequency and intensity of drinking, choices of alcoholic beverages, the locations of drinking, the purposes for drinking, and the effects of drinking) within and across Native tribes as between Native People as a whole and other racial/cultural groups (Levy and Kunitz, 1974; Stratton, et al, 1978; Fisher, 1984; Westermeyer, 1972, 1984; Leland, 1981).   There are Native tribes that have low rates of alcohol problems and alcoholism and many Native Americans who have a trouble-free relationship with alcohol (Westermeyer, 1974).   Also noteworthy are the findings that Native people who are racially mixed have the same or a higher prevalence of alcohol problems than Natives of greater "racial purity" (Lemert, 1982).

One of the most recent scientific reviews of genetic factors in Native alcohol problems concluded:

> *Decades of research have failed to establish a purely Indian component to vulnerability to alcoholism....* (Long, et al., 2002).

Differences in alcoholism rates within and between tribes reflect not differences in racial biology, but variations in individual vulnerability as well as the extent to which cultural cohesion within tribes serves as a preventive shield and healing force. Biological vulnerability to alcoholism is intergenerationally transmitted within particular families, but there is no evidence that this biological vulnerability differs by race. Reviewing the historical and scientific evidence, Dwight Heath concluded that the "stereotype of the 'drunken Indian' is not generally accurate today, and appears never to have been in history" (Heath, 1983, p. 383).   In seeking to understand the roots of alcohol problems in Native America, one would be better served by a text on Native American history than a text on the bio-genetics of alcoholism.

Fact Four: The solutions to Native alcohol problems lie within Native communities. Most of the coming chapters will detail the historical evidence to support this conclusion. Solutions to Native alcohol problems that have come from the dominant culture have long constituted a type of "poisoned medicine" that masks their harmful long-term effects in words of great promise. Even the most well-intentioned efforts of outsiders to intervene in Native alcohol problems have often further disempowered these communities by implying that the source of these problems lie within Native communities while the solutions to these problems can only be found outside these communities.

Solutions to alcohol problems from outside Native cultures reinforce the very anomie and hopelessness that feed these problems. For example, the federal prohibition of the sale of alcohol to Indians from 1832 to 1953 reinforced the view that Native People were more vulnerable to alcoholism than whites, and less able to care for these problems within their own cultures (Hassrick, 1947). What modern evaluations of interventions into alcohol problems in Native communities conclude is that the most successful of these interventions are 1) generated from within tribal communities, 2) utilize indigenous role models of recovery and sobriety, 3) utilize culturally specific pathways and tools for long-term recovery, 4) create a sustainable community of recovery, and 5) link personal recovery to the larger umbrella of community renewal and health (Long, et al, 2002; Coyhis and White, 2003).

The Function of Firewater Myths

If there is no historical or scientific evidence to support the firewater myths, one is left questioning the source of their origin and their persistence. To do this requires an examination of the context in which these ideas arose and the functions they historically served and may continue to serve.

The firewater myths served a number of important functions. They:

1) helped establish and maintain systems of domination and subjugation by reinforcing views of European superiority and Native inferiority (Morgan, 1983);

2) reduced moral culpability of Euro-Americans by masking the larger political, economic and cultural conditions out of which Native alcohol problems arose and were sustained;

3) buttressed the vision of Manifest Destiny (controlling all lands "discovered" between the Atlantic and Pacific Oceans) by defining Native People as subhuman;

4) provided ideological justification for pre-emptive assaults upon and the enforced isolation of Native communities;

5) and justified a wide range of invasive, social control measures within Indian Country.

Words and ideas are important weapons of conquest, subjugation, and extermination. If you want to care for something, you call it a *flower*; if you want to kill something, you call it a *weed*. The firewater myths were part of a larger process of dehumanization that rendered Native Peoples a *weed* in the eyes of Euro-Americans. William Gilmore Simms described this process in 1845.

> *It* [failure to recognize the intelligence and skill of Native leaders] *is only to be accounted for by reference to our blinding prejudices against the race-- prejudices which seem to have been fostered as necessary to justify the reckless and unsparing hand with which we have smitten them in their habitations, and expelled them from their country. We must prove them unreasoning beings, to sustain our pretensions as human ones, show them to have been irreclaimable, to maintain our own claims to the regards and respect of civilization* (Simms, 1845, p. 359).

THE

SPEECH

OF A

CREEK-INDIAN,

AGAINST THE

IMMODERATE USE

OF

SPIRITUOUS LIQUORS.

DELIVERED

In a National Affembly of the *Creeks*, upon
the breaking out of the late WAR.

To which are added,

1. A LETTER from YARIZA, an *Indian*
Maid of the Royal Line of the *Mohawks*, to
the principal Ladies of *New York*. 2. INDIAN
Songs of Peace. 3. An AMERICAN *Fable*.

Together with

Some REMARKS upon the Characters and
Genius of the *Indians*, and upon their Cuftoms
and Ceremonies at making War and Peace.

*Viri Ninivitæ, & REGINA Auftri, exfurgent in judicio
cum viris hujus gentis, & condemnabunt eos.*
———*Nec longum tempus, et ingens
Exiit ad cælum, ramis felicibus, arbos.*

LONDON:

Printed for R. GRIFFITHS, Bookfeller, in *St. Paul's
Church-Yard.* M.DCC.LIV.

The title page of a pamphlet published in London in 1754. This passionate
oration shows that Native People spoke out against the use of alcohol among
their own people from before the Founding of the American Nation. In this
speech, the Native orator says, "(Liquor) perverts the ends of society, and unfits
us for all those distinguishing and exquisite *Feelings,* which are the Cordials of
Life, and the noblest Privileges of *Humanity*" (Mancall, 1995, p.187). Courtesy
Houghton Library, Harvard University.

Exaggerating Native alcohol problems, misrepresenting the source of these problems as one of racial taint and portraying Native cultures as incapable of resolving their own problems served multiple functions, but played a particularly important role in undermining tribal sovereignty. Mosher notes how the federal government used alcohol problems to translate "its power to regulate trade with the tribes into a power to regulate the lives of individual Indians" (Mosher, 1975, p. 16). The resulting laws and policies undermined the autonomy and political sovereignty of the tribes and defined Indian People as dependent wards of the federal government.

Perhaps more than any other investigator, Patricia Morgan (1983) has unraveled the role alcohol can play in establishing and sustaining patterns of domination and subordination. This is done by shaping perceptions of alcohol's effects on particular populations, by promoting alcohol intoxication to dissipate political protest and maintain a population's subjugated status, by paternalistically controlling the supply of alcohol, and by asserting mechanisms of social control via the rationale of controlling alcohol problems.

The firewater myths have long served as part of the machinery of cultural domination and subjugation. By defining Native Peoples as something less than human, these myths helped people who saw themselves as good Christians participate in, or silently condone, the attempted extermination of an entire race of people. Contemporary discussions that portray Native alcohol problems as a racial taint, while avoiding the historical context of these problems, reflect a continuation of that tradition.

Both this larger construction of the idea of "Indian," and the more specific construction of firewater myths provided the ideological justification for the exploitation and extermination of Native tribes. The Indian was to be destroyed physically or destroyed through assimilation. The former would open the frontier and the latter, through the process of detribalization, would eliminate group claims for land as well as demands for redress of historical grievances. Alcohol contributed to the physical decimation of

Native Peoples, and, by contributing to cultural disruption, also served as a tool of detribalization.

Firewater Myths and Native Peoples

The tragedy of the firewater myths is not simply in its wide inculcation among members of the dominant culture. The greatest tragedy is that so many Native People have themselves come to believe these propositions. The firewater myths have had a number of destructive effects on Native Peoples over the past 300 years.

First, they impact how Native People see themselves as a people. The perception of rampant alcoholism in Native communities and the paternalistic, external control measures generated in response to this perception, have served as stigmatizing reminders of the inferior and dependent status of Native Peoples.

Second, the firewater myths impact how individual Native People view their own relationship with alcohol. The firewater myths and their accompanying caricature (the "drunken Indian") virtually ignored (and continue to ignore) Indians who abstained from drinking alcohol and those who drank in moderation (Mancall, 1993). The effects of social labeling and self-perception are very powerful, e.g., kids labeled "bad" kids or "smart" kids tend to act in conformity to these labels. The constant linkage made between Native drinking and alcoholism may exert its own expectancy effect that increases Native drinking problems. When you keep hearing these myths, and hearing them, and hearing them, and hearing them, and hearing them, and hearing them wherever you go, you start to believe that they are true. American Indians didn't start these lies, but Native societies have believed them and spread them. The first thing Native Peoples must do in addressing alcohol problems in our communities is to discover the truth about the source of these problems, and that discovery begins by exposing the lies that make up the firewater myths.

Third, the firewater myths and external suppression of alcohol use has transformed alcohol into a symbol of cultural protest that paradoxically generates a pattern of defiant self-destruction. Nancy Oestreich Lurie has proposed that efforts to impose sobriety from outside Native cultures inadvertently created a climate in which drinking became a form of protest and a means of asserting one's Indianhood (Lurie, 1974). It is in this historical context that sobriety is today being redefined as an act of cultural resistance linked to tribal identity and political sovereignty. Destructive drinking is not a reflection of or an affirmation of one's *Indianness*. To drink in this manner is to embrace a lie about oneself and one's people. Seen in this context, intoxication is not an act of protest, but an act of personal and cultural suicide. Seen in this context, recovery and sobriety become acts of personal and cultural defiance--a refusal to have one's power neutralized by potions, pills or powders. What the coming chapters will illustrate is that sobriety, not drunkenness, is the Indian way.

The "firewater myths" are not historical artifacts: they continue to operate today. The persistence of these myths suggests that evolving interests may still be served by such racial stereotypes (Holmes and Antell, 2001). It may still be easier for America at large to talk about Native vulnerability to alcoholism as a biologically-based phenomenon than to talk about Native alcoholism in the context of historical trauma (Brave Heart, 2003). The slaughter of Native Peoples, loss of Native lands, forced migration, grinding poverty, malnutrition, and continued government intrusion into Native family and tribal life are more accurate causes of Indian alcoholism than the biological explanation. The firewater myths continue to provide a conscience-salving escape from accountability and an unstated rationale for continued neglect. It is possible, as Levy and Kunitz suggest, that these myths continue to underlie inadequate funding for the prevention and treatment of Native alcohol problems and the broader investment in Native communities (Levy and Kunitz, 1974). Debunking these myths will require viewing Native alcohol problems in the historical and cultural contexts out of which they arose and have endured. It will require revealing the untold story of Native People's relationship with alcohol: the story of resistance and recovery.

References

Abbott, P.J. (1998). Traditional and western healing practices for alcoholism in American Indians and Alaskan Natives. *Substance Use and Misuse, 33*(13):2605-2646.

Berkhofer, R. (1979). *The White Man's Indian: Images of the American Indian from Columbus to the Present.* New York: Vintage.

Berreman, G.D. (1956). Drinking patterns of the Aleuts. *Quarterly Journal of Studies on Alcohol, 17*:503-515.

Brave Heart, M.Y.H. (2003). The historical trauma response among Natives and its relationship with substance abuse: A Lakota illustration. *Journal of Psychoactive Drugs*, 35(1), 7-13.

Coyhis, D. and White, W. (2003). Alcohol problems in Native America: Changing paradigms and clinical practices. *Alcoholism Treatment Quarterly, 3/4*:157-165.

Dailey, R.C. (1979). The role of alcohol among North American Indian tribes as reported in "The Jesuit Relations." In, Marshall, M. Ed. *Beliefs, Behaviors and Alcoholic Beverages.* Ann Arbor: University of Michigan Press.

Fisher, A.D. (1984). Alcoholism and race: The misapplication of both concepts to North American Native Americans. *Canadian Review of Sociology and Anthropology, 24*(1):81-98.

French, L.A. (2000). *Addictions and Native Americans.* Westport, CT: Praeger.

Garcia-Andrade, C., Wall, T. and Ehlers, C. (1997). The firewater myth and response to alcohol in Mission Indians. *American Journal of Psychiatry, 154*(7):983-8.

Hassrick, R. (1947). Alcohol and Indians. *The American Indians, 4*(2):19-26.

Hawkins, H.H. and Blume, A.W. (2002). Loss of sacredness: Historical context of health policies for Indigenous People in the United States. In Mail, P. Herutin-Roberts, S, Martcin, S., and Howard, J. Eds. *Alcohol Use Among American Indians and Alaskan Natives* (NIAAA

Research Monograph No. 37). Bethesda, MD: National Institute in Alcohol Abuse and Alcoholism, pp. 25-46.

Heath, D. (1983). Alcohol use among North American Indians: A cross-cultural survey of patterns and problems. In: *Research Advances in Alcohol and Drug Problems, Volume 7,* Ed. By Reginald Smart, et.al., NY: Plenum Press, pp. 343-396.

Holmes, M and Antell, J. (2001). The social construction of American Indian drinking: Perceptions of American Indian and White officials. *The Sociological Quarterly, 42*(2):151-173.

Leland, J. (1981). The context of Native American drinking: What we know so far. *NIAAA Res. Monogr. Series, 7*:173-205.

Lemert, E.M. (1982). Drinking among American Indians. In: Gomberg, E.L., White, H.R., and Carpenter, J.A., Eds., *Alcohol, Science, and Society Revisited.* New Brunswick, NJ: Rutgers Center of Alcohol Studies, pp. 80-95.

Levy, J.E. and Kunitz, S.J. (1974). *Indian Drinking: Navajo Practices and Anglo-American Theories,* New York: Wiley.

Long, J.C., Mail, P.D., Thomasson, H.R. (2002). Genetic susceptibility and alcoholism in American Indians. In Mail, P. Herutin-Roberts, S, Martcin, S., and Howard, J. Eds. *Alcohol Use Among American Indians and Alaskan Natives,* (NIAAA Research Monograph No. 37). Bethesda, MD: National Institute on Alcohol Abuse and Alcoholism, pp. 71-86.

Lurie, N. (1974). The world's oldest on-going protest demonstration: North American Indian drinking patterns In: Hundley, N. Ed. *The American Indian.* Santa Barbara, California: CLIO Books, pp.55-76.

Macleod, W.C. (1928). *The American Indian Frontier.* New York: Alfred A. Knopf.

Mancall. P. (1993). "The bewitching tyranny of custom": The social costs of Indian drinking in colonial America. *American Indian Culture and Research Journal, 17*(2):15-42.

Mancall, P. (1995). *Deadly Medicine: Indians and Alcohol in Early America.* Ithaca, NY: Cornell University Press.

Mancall, P. (1997). *"I was addicted to rum": Four Centuries of Alcohol Consumption In Indian Country.* Presented at Historical Perspectives on Drug and Alcohol Use in American Society, 1800-1997. College of Physicians of Philadelphia, May 9-11.

May, P. (1977). Explanations of Native American drinking. *Plains Anthropologist, 22*(77):223-232.

May, P. (1989). That was yesterday, and (hopefully) yesterday is gone. *American Indian and Alaska Native Mental Health Research, 2*(3):71-74.

May, P. (1994). The epidemiology of alcohol abuse among American Indians: The mythical and real Properties. *American Indian Culture and Research Journal, 18:*121-143.

Mitchell, C.M., Beals, J., Novins, D.K., & Spicer, P. (2003). Drug use among two American Indian populations: Prevalence of lifetimes use and DSM-IV substance use disorders. *Drug and Alcohol Dependence,* 69, 29-41.

Morgan, P. (1983). Alcohol, disinhibition, and domination: A conceptual analysis. In *Alcohol and Disinhibition: Nature and Meaning of the Link,* Ed. by Room and Collins. Washington D.C.: U.S. Government Printing Office.

Mosher, J. (1975). *Liquor Legislation and Native Americans: History and Perspective.* Working Paper F 136. Berkely: Social Research Group, University of California.

Schaefer, J.M. (1981). Firewater myths revisited: Review of findings and some new directions. In Heath, D.B.; Waddell, J.O.; and Topper, M.D., Eds. Cultural Factors in Alcohol Research and Treatment of Drinking Problems. *Journal of Studies on Alcohol Supplement, 9*:99-1171.

Simms, W.G. (1845). "The Noble North American Indian" In Butcher, P., Ed. (1977) *The Minority Presence in American Literature, 1600-1900, Volume One.* Washington, D.C.: Howard University Press, pp. 357-359.

Spicer, P., Beals, J., Croy, C., Mitchell, C., Novins, D., Moore, L., and Manson, S. (2003). The prevalence of DSM-III-R Alcohol

Dependence in Two American Indian Populations. *Alcoholism: Clinical and Experimental Research, 27*(11), 1785-1797.

Stratton, R., Zeiner, A., and Paredes, A. (1978). Tribal affiliation and prevalence of alcohol problems. *Journal of Studies on Alcohol, 39*:1166-1177.

Weibel-Orlando, J. (1986-1987). Drinking patterns of urban and rural American Indians. *Alcohol Health and Research World,* Winter, pp. 8-13.

Weibel-Orlando, J. (1990). American Indians and prohibition: Effect or affect? Views from the reservation and the city. *Contemporary Drug Problems, 17*(2):293-322.

Westermeyer, J. (1972). Options regarding alcohol use among the Chippewa. *American Journal of Orthopsychiatry, 42*(3):398-403.

Westermeyer, J. (1974). "The Drunken Indian:" Myths and realities. *Psychiatric Annals,* 4(11):29-36.

Westermeyer, J. (1984). The role of ethnicity in substance abuse. In: Stimmel, B., Ed., *Cultural and Sociological Aspects of Alcoholism and Substance Abuse.* New York: Haworth Press, pp. 9-18.

Westermeyer, J. (1988). The Pursuit of intoxication: Our 100 century-old romance with psychoactive substances. *American Journal of Drug and Alcohol Abuse,* 14:175-187.

Westermeyer, J. and Baker, J. (1986). Alcoholism and the American Indian. In N.S. Estes and M.E. Heineman (Eds.) *Alcoholism: Development, Consequences, and Interventions.* 3rd edition, pp. 273-282. St. Louis: Mosby.

Womak, M.L. (1996). *The Indianization of Alcoholics Anonymous: An examination of Native American recovery movements.* Master's thesis, Department of American Indian Studies, University of Arizona.

Part Two: Early Resistance and Recovery

Recovery is like a fire; someone has to start it.
—From *The Honour of All,*
the 1985 Alkali Lake Video

The community is the treatment center
—Andy Chelsea
Shuswap Tribal Chief
From the Alkali Lake Video

Andy Chelsea (left), Pat Martel, and Francois Paulette in a 1985
photograph at a community development workshop on the Hay River
First Nations Reserve, Canada.

Chapter Five

Native Responses to Alcohol and Alcoholism:
An Overview

The history of early Native American responses to rising alcohol-related problems is usually pictured as a crusade by cultural outsiders (white missionaries and politicians) to impose sobriety on an intemperate race. This image is challenged by the historical facts. Native People and tribes were not passive victims of alcohol-related problems. They responded to growing alcohol problems on multiple fronts: through the family, through the use of Native medicine, through political advocacy and through Native religious and cultural revitalization movements. In fact, these responses were highly integrated. The familial, cultural, religious, political and medical were not separate spheres of life for Native Americans. It was not unusual for chiefs to also be medicine men (e.g., Sitting Bull, Joseph, Geronimo, and Cochise) and many of the religious leaders we will profile were also political leaders and healers (Vogel, 1970).

Adaptations to the troublesome effects of alcohol followed the first availability of alcohol. In some tribes, Native drinkers gave up their weapons to other tribal or family members who pledged not to drink as a precaution against injury and harm while drinking (Dailey, 1979). Native women sought to reduce the casualties resulting from communal sprees by hiding weapons, their children and themselves (Mancall, 1995). Native women and children bore much of the brunt of male intoxication and quickly found ways to ameliorate this problem.

Native healers sought to treat alcoholism. In many tribes, such healers were called to their roles by having suffered through illness and having gained knowledge of how to master it (Kehoe, 1989). One of the earliest sources of the very idea of "wounded healer"--the notion that people who have faced and overcome adversity might have special sensitivities and skills in helping others experiencing the same adversity--springs from this Native tradition. It is within this tradition that Native healers--many who overcame their own problems with alcohol--forged frameworks to heal individuals, families and tribes who had been wounded by alcohol problems and alcoholism. These frameworks included healing rituals and Native medicines that served to counter both the craving for alcohol and the effects of alcohol. Early Native treatments for alcoholism included Hop Tea, used in some tribes in the belief that it reduced craving, and the root of the Trumpet Vine which served as a deterrent to drinking by producing a reaction similar to disulfram (Antabuse) (Scully, 1970; Cohen, 1985).

When alcohol problems transcended the management capacities of family and medicine people, it was Native political leaders, not local white officials or missionaries, who demanded political action to stop the liquor trading practices (Bordewich, 1996). In 1701, Delaware and Shawnee chiefs visited the Governor of Pennsylvania to protest the presence of traders who would bring as many as 150 gallons of rum to their villages and then take everything from those intoxicated, including the clothes they were wearing (Cherrington, 1925-26). In 1738, local Shawnee chiefs presented the following resolution to Pennsylvania authorities that was signed by one hundred warriors:

This day we have held a council, and it is agreed by the Shawnee in general that whatever rum is in our towns shall be broke and spilt and not drunk; and whoever shall bring any rum or any sort of strong drink into our towns, Indian or white man, let it be little or much, it shall be broke or spilt in the presence of the whole town... (Quoted in Macleod, 1928, p. 37).

During this same period, the Iroquois announced that they would destroy the liquor of any trader who opened their supplies of it within Iroquois territory (Macleod, 1928). A century later, in his 1833 autobiography, Black Hawk (Ma-ka-tai-me-she-kia-kiak) described the use of similar tactics to stop drunkenness among his tribe.

The white people brought whiskey into our village, made our people drunk, and cheated them out of their horses, guns, and traps!...I visited all the whites and begged them not to sell whiskey to my people. One of them continued the practice openly. I took a party of my young men, went to his house, and took his barrel and broke in the head and turned out the whiskey (quoted in Apess, 1833, p. 161).

There were tribes like the Cree who refused to accept alcohol as a token of trade, on the grounds that alcohol warranted nothing of value in trade (Hamer and Steinbring, 1980).

Black Snake, a 97 year old Seneca chief, made the following plea to white officials on September 4, 1845:

But who is it that has made my people drunk? Indians cannot make whiskey. Indians do not sell it. But white people make it and bring it among us. It is they that have brought the evil upon us and we cannot remove it. The white people can remove it and now we call upon them to do it. We ask them to take their whiskey and run away, and leave us sober as they found us (quoted in Cherrington, 1925-26, p. 21).

Like Black Snake, many tribal leaders spoke out against alcohol. The chiefs of the Comanches, a tribe widely known for their temperance, branded alcohol as "fools water." When the English sent a cask of rum to the Cayugas just before they were to meet in council, the chiefs returned the cask with a note that said:

We have drunk too much of your rum already, which has occasioned our destruction; we will, in the future, beware of it (Cherrington, 1925-26, pp. 6,16).

In the face of non-enforcement of liquor laws, Native leaders evolved their own internal systems of law and punishment. Estamaza, Chief of the Omahas, dramatically reduced drunkenness by implementing severe penalties (whippings, beatings, destruction of property) upon those bringing alcohol into tribal land (Johnson, 1911). Native leaders, recognizing the role alcohol was playing in treaty negotiations, also rejected gifts of alcohol and requested that alcohol not be provided during or after political negotiations (Unrau, 1996).

Native leaders became increasingly involved in political advocacy to stop the exploitive alcohol trafficking in Indian territories, some even going as far as raiding and destroying the supplies of whiskey traders. Tribal chiefs such as Tecumseh, Sitting Bull, and Crazy Horse voiced strong opposition to the use of alcohol and were successful in getting laws passed banning or restricting the whisky traffic in Indian Country. These laws, the first of which was passed in Massachusetts in 1633, usually went unenforced (Lewis, 1982; Cherrington, 1920; Daniels, 1877; Dacus, 1877). Native efforts to negotiate a ban on the liquor traffic within treaties began with a Choctaw Nation treaty of 1820, but such efforts failed from lack of enforcement (Johnson, 1911). The extent of such non-enforcement is well-illustrated by a case of bootlegging in which the jury, to assure that confiscated bottles actually contained alcohol, sampled them repeatedly until the case had to be dismissed because all of the evidence was gone (Anderson, 1988).

One of the most articulate champions against the liquor traffic was the Miami Chief Meshekinoquah (Mechecunnaqua, Little Turtle) who waged a relentless effort before various state legislatures to stem the flow of alcohol into Indian Country. The following are excerpts from a speech he gave to a Quaker meeting in Baltimore in 1801:

> *When our forefathers first met on this island, your red brethren were more numerous; but since the introduction amongst us, of what you call spirituous liquors, and what we think may justly be called poison, our numbers have greatly diminished...It is not an evil of our own making; we have not placed it amongst ourselves; it is an evil placed amongst us by white people* (Quoted in Johnson, 1911, pp. 175-176).

Meshekinoquah went on to describe the effects of the liquor trade on Native men and their families:

> *After repeated offers, ...one finally accepts it and takes a drink, and getting one he wants another, and then a third and fourth till his senses have left him. After reason comes back to him, he gets up and finds where he is. He asks for his peltry. The answer is, you have drank them. Where is my gun? It is gone. Where is my blanket? You have sold it for whiskey. Now, brothers, figure to yourself what a condition this man must be in--he has a family at home, a wife and children that stand in need of the profits of his hunting. What*

must their wants be, when he is even without a shirt?
(Quoted in Johnson, 1911, p. 176-177).

William Johnson, in his 1911 study of the federal government's response to the liquor traffic, notes the historical significance of Meshekinoquah's work: "The fact that he wore feathers instead of a silk hat may, in part, account for his not having been given the place in the history of temperance reform that his works justly entitle him to" (Johnson, 1911, p. 180).

The journals of the Jesuit missionaries record the following words of Abenakis to the English authorities:

Thou deputy of Pleimont and Boston, paint our words on paper and send them to those on whom thou are dependent; and say to them that all the allied Savages dwelling on the river Kenebek hate fire-water...; and that if they (the English) have any more of it brought hither to sell to the Savages, the latter will believe the English wish to exterminate them (Quoted in Dailey, 1979).

Some tribes responded to the growing presence of alcohol by absorbing alcohol into their cultures and forming rules designed to maximize its benefits and minimize its harmful effects on individuals and on the tribe as a whole. This cultural rulemaking was an extension of the ritualized controls that had worked well to limit psychoactive drug use before European contact. This strategy had several limitations. First, alcohol was arriving in a highly potent form unknown to most Native tribes and it was arriving in enormous quantities. Second, models were not widely available for the ritualized, moderate use of alcohol. And most importantly, the power of Native cultures to shape their members' behavior was weakening under the forces of mass death, dislocation and demoralization.

Native medicine and spiritual, cultural revitalization, as well as indigenous healing movements grew in importance as solutions to alcohol-related personal, family and political problems. Healing movements such as the Handsome Lake Movement, the Indian Shaker Church, and the Native American Church called for a return to Native traditions and demanded total abstinence from alcohol (Weibel-Orlando, 1989). These sobriety-based religious and cultural revitalization movements were often founded by individuals who had themselves suffered from alcoholism.

These movements strengthened tribal traditions and provided a preventive shield and a curative framework for alcoholism. They provided sobriety-based belief systems, sobriety-based social networks, and sobriety-based rituals of daily living. While Native efforts to respond to rising problems with alcohol were compromised as these movements came under attack and were engulfed in a larger and more sustained efforts to eliminate Native religion and culture (Cooley, 1980), these movements constitute the earliest alcoholism recovery support structures in America. This story begins in the early eighteenth century—more than 200 years before the founding of Alcoholics Anonymous. In the coming chapters, we will catalogue the leaders, movements, ideas and events that make up the early history of Native American recovery.

References

Abbott, P.J. (1998). Traditional and western healing practices for alcoholism in American Indians and Alaskan Natives. *Substance Use and Misuse, 33*(13):2605-2646.

Anderson, T.I. (1988). *Alaska Hooch.* Fairbanks, AK: Hoo-Che-Noo.

Apes, W. (1829). *A Son of the Forest. The Experience of William Apes, A Native of the Forest, Comprising a Notice of the Pequod Tribe of Indians, Written by Himself.* New York: By the Author.

Bordewich, F. (1996). *Killing the White Man's Indian.* New York: Anchor Books.

Cherrington, E. (1920). *The Evolution of Prohibition in the United States.* Westerville, Ohio: The American Issue Press.

Cherrington, E. (1925-1926). Ed. *Standard Encyclopedia of the Alcohol Problem,* (Six Volumes). Westerville, Ohio, American Issue Publishing Company.

Cohen, S. (1985). *The Substance Abuse Problems: New Issues for the 1980s.* New York, NY: The Haworth Press.

Dacus, J. (1877). *Battling with the Demon: The Progress of Temperance.* Saint Louis, MO: Scammell & Company.

Dailey, R.C. (1979). The role of alcohol among North American Indian tribes as reported in "The Jesuit Relations." In, Marshall, M. Ed.. *Beliefs, Behaviors and Alcoholic Beverages.* Ann Arbor: University of Michigan Press.

Daniels, W. (1877). *The Temperance Reform and Its Great Reformers.* NY: Nelson and Phillips).

Hamer, J. and Steinbring, J. Eds. (1980). *Alcohol and Native Peoples of the North.* Washington, D.C.: University Press of America.

Johnson, W.E. (1911). *The Federal Government and the Liquor Traffic.* Westerville, Ohio: The American Issue Publishing Company.

Kehoe, A. (1989). *The Ghost Dance: Ethnohistory and Revitalization.* New York: Holt, Rinehart and Winston.

Lewis, R. (1982). Alcoholism and the Native American: A review of the literature. In Alcohol and Health Monograph 4: Special Population Issues. NIAAA, U.S. Government Printing.

Macleod, W.C. (1928). *The American Indian Frontier.* New York: Alfred A. Knopf.

Mancall, P. (1995). *Deadly Medicine: Indians and Alcohol in Early America.* Ithaca, NY: Cornell University Press.

Niehardt, J.G. (1932, 1961). *Black Elk Speaks.* Lincoln: University of Nebraska Press.

Scully, V. (1970). *A Treasury of American Indian Herbs.* NY: Crown Publishers, Inc.

Unrau, William (1996). *White Man's Wicked Water: The Alcohol Trade and Prohibition in Indian Country, 1802-1892.* Lawrence: University Press of Kansas.

Vogel, V. (1970). *American Indian Medicine.* Norman, Oklahoma: University of Oklahoma Press.

Weibel-Orlando, J. (1989). Treatment and prevention of Native American alcoholism in Watts, T. and Wright, R. Eds. (1989). *Alcoholism in Minority Populations.* Springfield, Illinois: Charles C. Thomas.

Chapter Six

The Delaware Prophets

As early as 1737, a Native "seer" preached to the Shawnee and Onondaga that they were being punished for their love of rum-- that the Great Spirit had taken their game as punishment for their drunkenness (Cave, 1999). This spotlight on alcohol by Native religious leaders intensified in the 1740s, particularly among the Delaware Indians who had lost most of their ancestral lands and who were described at the time as "drunken, disillusioned, dependent, and hostile--a people in limbo" (Wallace, 1956).

The Lenni Lenape Indians, widely known as the Delaware, experienced extreme cultural disruption in the mid-eighteenth century. Anglo-American encroachment on tribal lands had created a western-moving refugee community within the Ohio and Allegheny River Valleys. It was in the midst of such disruption that six prophets emerged between 1744 and 1766 to launch abstinence-based cultural revitalization movements among the Delaware. What written records we have of these prophetic movements come from the journals of white missionaries and travelers (Brainerd, 1822 and Zeisberger, 1910, 1912).

These cultural revitalization movements marked a shift in identity through which Native Peoples shifted from seeing themselves in terms of tribal identities and rivalries to a larger recognition of themselves as a race of people in a shared struggle for survival against Anglo-American assault and colonization (Dowd, 1992a; Gilmour, 1992). It was in this new worldview that the Delaware prophets conceptualized alcohol as a weapon of cultural assault, called for its rejection (along with the rejection of other trappings of Anglo-American culture), and advocated a return to Native beliefs and traditions. While the prophet movements were political and cultural revitalization movements, they were also personal reform movements through which many Native Americans suffering from alcoholism rejected alcohol and developed new sobriety-based identities.

In 1744, a prophet whose name is lost to history attributed the growing physical and cultural sickness among the Delaware to the loss of sacred traditions and the growing consumption of, and dependence upon, alcohol. The prophet in this early account called for a boycott of alcohol and all other Anglo-American goods and a return to traditional Native beliefs and practices (Wallace, 1956; Gilmour, 1992). In 1751, Wyoming Woman began preaching to the Delaware about "the poison among them."

In 1752, Papounhan (Papoonan), a Unami (Munsee) Delaware, who had long suffered from alcoholism, went into the forest for a period of sustained meditation following the death of his father. After sobering himself, he experienced a vision and returned to carry a message of personal reformation and return to cultural traditions. He called for a boycott on all trade with Anglo-Americans and chastised his Native listeners for emulating the greed of the white man. Papounhan and his followers were known as "Quaker Indians" (Cave, 1999; Hirschfelder and Molin, 2001; Dowd, 1992a). As late as 1760 they were described as "strictly adhering to the ancient Customs and Manners of their Forefathers" (Frederick Post, 1760, Quoted in Hunter, 1971, p. 42).

Wangomend (or Wangomen), known as the Assinsink Prophet (of the Assinsink Munsee Tribe), exhorted his tribe in 1752 to denounce rum, and threatened that those who did not would suffer in Hell. He created a "quarterly meeting" to reaffirm the commitment to sobriety. The meeting lasted for a full day and involved dream interpretation, walking, singing, dancing and cathartic weeping (Cave, 1999; Dowd, 1992a).

In 1755, Neolin (The Delaware Prophet, The Enlightened), the best known of the Delaware prophets, extended the separatist theology of Papounhan by calling upon the Delaware to give up the sins and vices that they had learned from white people (Cave, 1999). Using a chart that pictured rum as an obstacle on the path to Heaven, he called for the rejection of all alcohol and the substitution of the Black Drink (known across various tribes as asse, assinola, assini, cassena, yahola, or yopon) (Johnson, 1911). The Black Drink was a non-intoxicating tea made from the cassia plant (*Ilex vomitoria* plant) that induced vomiting (Safford, 1906; Wallace, 1956). Its ritual use to purify Native peoples of "White peoples ways and Nature" spread through many Appalachian tribes (Dowd, 1992a, p. 33).

It is in Neolin's preaching that we get the fullest development to date of an American Indian identity juxtaposed against an Anglo-American Identity. Neolin called upon Native People of all tribes to see themselves as a single race of people. He felt it was only by establishing unity as a race that all tribes would be able to prevent their physical and cultural destruction. The rejection of alcohol in all of its forms was a centerpiece of Neolin's teachings. In 1759, he conveyed the following words from the Master of Life to his Native audience:

> *Listen to that which I will tell thee for thyself and for all Indians. I am the Maker of Heaven and Earth, the trees, lakes, rivers, men, and all that thou seest or hast seen on the earth and in the heavens; and because I love you, you must do my will; you must also avoid that which I hate; I hate you*

to drink as you do, until you lose your reason...Hear what the Great Spirit has ordered me to tell you! You are to make sacrifices, in the manner that I shall direct; to put off entirely from yourselves the customs to which you have adopted since the white people came among us; you are to return to that former happy state, in which we lived in peace and plenty, before these strangers came to disturb us, and above all, you must abstain from drinking their deadly beson [liquor], which they forced upon us for the sake of increasing their gains and diminishing our numbers (Wallace, 1969, p. 117, 120).

Neolin condemned polygamy, promiscuity and witchcraft as well as drunkenness. He called for Indian unity, cultural purification and personal purification--the latter acquired through rejection of alcohol, sexual abstinence, and the ritual use of the Black Drink. Both Wangomen and Neolin introduced the use of an "Indian Bible"--a fifteen-inch-square, lined map that dramatized the Indian pathway to the "Heavenly regions" (Hays, 1954 and Kenney, 1913). The final Delaware prophet of this period was Scattameck who in 1771 called upon Indian people to replace the white man's rum with a drink made from herbs and roots, to reject white ways of thinking and living, and to return to the Indian way (Dowd, 1992a).

The Delaware prophets championed a sobriety-based, intertribal identity and offered new Native religions in direct competition to Christianity. They claimed that the white man and his religion were suspect due to the enslavement of blacks, the assault on Native Peoples and the theft of Native lands. The prophets appropriated the concepts of a punishing deity and heaven and hell and reframed them in a Native theology that incorporated many traditional beliefs and rituals. The prophets used these concepts to link alcohol to the individual and collective destruction of Native People. As Neolin warned:

"...if you suffer the Englishmen to dwell in your midst, their diseases and poisons shall destroy you utterly and you shall die" (Cherrington, 1926, p. 17).

What the Delaware prophets collectively offered was a way to understand personal and cultural defeat, a framework for personal recovery and cultural revitalization, and hope for the future for individuals and for a people (Cave, 1999).

Oddiduo

Preparing the Black Drink. The "Black Drink," made from leaves of yaupan holly, was drunk by Native People of the southeast both prior to and after European contact. It was used ceremonially and had purifying emetic effects on the drinker. It is a plant-based psychoactive drug that was used in a sacred manner. From a painting by Johan von Staden (Frankfurt, 1592). Courtesy, Library Company of Philadelphia.

References

Brainerd, D. (1822). *Memoirs of the Rev. David Brainerd.* Edited by Jonathon Edwards. New Haven: Converse.

Cave, A. The Delaware Prophet Neolin: A reappraisal. *Ethnohistory, 46*(2):265-290.

Dowd, G.E. (1992a). *A Spirited Resistance: The North American Indian Struggle for Unity: 1745-1815.* Baltimore, MD: John Hopkins University Press.

Gilmour, R. (1992). *Prophets and Refugees: The Development of a Pan-Indian Identity 1744-1765.* http://www.yorku.ca/ghistory/rgilmore/ithink/academic/papers/panid.htm, Accessed September 30, 2001.

Hays, J. (1954). John Hays' diary and journal of 1760. *Pennsylvania Archeologist, 24*(2):63-84. Homeside: Society for Pennsylvania Archeology.

Hirschfelder, A. and Molin, P. (2001). *Encyclopedia of Native American Religion.* New York: Checkmark Books.

Hunter, C. (1971). The Delaware Nativist revival of the mid-eighteenth century. *Ethnohistory, 18*:39-49.

Johnson, W.E. (1911). *The Federal Government and the Liquor Traffic.* Westerville, Ohio: The American Issue Publishing Company.

Kenney, J. (1913). Journal of James Kenny, 1761-1763. *Pennsylvania Magazine of History and Biography, 37*:1-201. Philadelphia: Historical Society of Pennsylvania.

Wallace, A. (1956). New religious beliefs among the Delaware Indians, 1600-1900. *Southwestern Journal of Anthropology, 12*:1-21.

Wallace, A. (1969). *The Death and Rebirth of the Seneca.* New York: Vintage Books.

Zeisberger, D. (1910). David Zeisberger's history of northern American Indiana. *Ohio Archeological and Historical Quarterly, 19*:1-189.

Chapter Seven

Redemption and Recovery: The Indian Preachers

Between 1730 and 1770, and again between 1790 and 1840, America experienced two Great Awakenings--periods of religious fervor spawned by itinerant preachers whose powerful extemporaneous sermons swelled membership in the Presbyterian, Methodist, Baptist and Congregationalist churches. Preachers such as Jonathon Edwards turned sermons with titles like "Sinners in the Hands of an Angry God" (Edwards, J., 1741) into emotionally charged theatrical performances that shifted the religious center of the country.

Native People who converted to Christianity during these periods and went on to become preachers created a unique brand and style of Christian healing sect whose hybridized beliefs and rituals provided a framework for personal recovery from alcohol problems and alcoholism for many Native People. Many Native tribes of the East (the Iroquois, Choctaw, Creek, Cherokee, Shawnee and Kickapoo) successfully incorporated social and religious sanctions against drinking through various forms of Native Christianity (Thomas, 1981). We will illustrate the earliest of such Christian recovery groups through the lives and work of two men: Samson Occom and William Apess.

Reverend Samson Occom, Mohegan, (1723-1792) was an American Indian Christian preacher who worked for recovery from alcohol among his Indian people, as well as condemning racial intolerance, which he says corrupts the minds of both whites and Indians.
Courtesy Illinois Addiction Studies Archives

William Apess, Pequot, (1798-1839) was an American Indian Methodist Minister who lived and worked with the Mashpee Indians preaching temperance as key to salvation and Native self-determination.
Courtesy Illinois Addiction Studies Archives

Samson Occom was born in 1723 along the Mohegan/Thames River in Southern Connecticut. He was the grandson of Uncas, a revered Mohegan chief, lived in a wigwam and spoke his Native language as a child. The pivotal shift in his life occurred at age seventeen when Samson Occom converted to Christianity and subsequently came under the tutelage of Reverend Eleazar Wheelock. Because of the remarkable abilities of Occom, Wheeler went on to found the Indian Charity School (Szasz, 1994).

After having his talents as a gospel minister nurtured by Wheelock, Occom was ordained as a Presbyterian minister on August 29, 1759. He served in the roles of minister and schoolmaster for the Montauk Indians of Long Island during his earlier clerical years. Occom spoke his native language as well as English, but distinguished himself through his literacy in Greek, Latin, French and Hebrew. His story is also unique in that he preached hundreds of sermons, not only to his own people, but to white audiences in America, England and Scotland (Peyer, 1982; Love, 2000).

Samson Occom went through a period of disillusionment when the large sums of money he raised abroad for the purpose of Indian education were diverted to support white rather than Indian students at the newly opened Dartmouth College. Embittered, Occom refused to visit the campus his labors had endowed and remained forever suspicious of white people claiming to represent the best interests of the Indian (Szasz, 1994). He also discovered upon his return that the promised care of his family during his fund-raising travels had been neglected. It was during this period that Occom fell into a period of intemperance, later confessing to his church:

I have been shamefully overtaken with strong drink, by which I have greatly wounded the cause of God... (Love, 2000, p. 163).

Occom drew from this experience a passionate message to his people about the devastating effects of alcohol. Highlights from his most famous and widely reprinted sermon (*Sermon at the Execution of Moses Paul*)--delivered at the September 2, 1772 execution of an Indian convicted of murder while intoxicated--convey the flavor of his message:

> *There is a dreadful woe denounced from the Almighty against drunkards; and it is this sin, this abominable, this beastly and accursed sin of drunkenness, that has stript us of every desirable comfort in this life; by this we are poor and wretched; by this sin we have no name or credit with in the world with polite nations; for this sin we are despised in the world...And it is for...that accursed sin of drunkenness that we suffer every day...And our poor children are suffering every day for want of necessities of life...All this is for the love of strong drink* (Love, 2000, p. 171).

Occom went on to challenge his Native audience to "break off from your drunkenness" and promised, "believe in the Lord Jesus and you shall be saved"(Love, 2000, p. 173). Following this widely acclaimed address, Occom continued to preach a message of sobriety and salvation to Native communities and became an activist in suppressing the alcohol traffic among Native Peoples until his death on July 14, 1792 (Love, 2000; Peyer, 1982). Joseph Johnson, a young Mohegan whose religious conversion had rescued him from drunkenness, married Occom's daughter, Tabitha, and carried forward Occom's work as a minister and schoolmaster (Szasz, 1994).

Mr. Occom's Addrefs
TO HIS
INDIAN BRETHREN.

On the Day that MOSES PAUL, an Indian, was executed at NEW-HAVEN, on the 2d of SEPTEMBER, 1772, for the Murder of MOSES COOK.

I.
MY kindred Indians, pray attend and hear,
With great attention and with godly fear;
This day I warn you of that curfed fin,
That poor, defpifed Indians wallow in.

II.
'Tis drunkennefs, this is the fin you know,
Has been and is poor Indians overthrow;
'Twas drunkennefs that was the leading caufe,
That made poor Mofes break God's righteous Laws.

III.
When drunk he other evil courfes took,
Thus hurried on, he murdered Mofes Cook;
Poor Mofes Paul muft now be hang'd this day,
For wilful murder in a drunken fray.

IV.
A dreadful wo pronounc'd by God on high,
To all that in this fin do lie;
O devilifh beaftly luft, accurfed fin,
Has almoft ftript us all of every thing.

V.
We've nothing valuable or to our praife,
And well may other nations on us gaze;
We have no money, credit or a name,
But what this fin does turn to our great fhame.

VI.
Mean are our houfes, and we are kept low,
And almoft naked, fhivering we go;
Pinch'd for food and almoft ftarv'd we are,
And many times put up with ftinking fare.

VII.
Our little children hovering round us weep,
Moft ftarv'd to death we've nought for them to eat;
All this diftrefs is juftly on us come,
For the accurfed ufe we make of rum.

VIII.
A fhocking, dreadful fight we often fee,
Our children young and tender, drunkards be;
More fhocking yet and awful to behold,
Our women will get drunk both young and old.

IX.
Behold a drunkard in a drunken fit,
Incapable to go, ftand, fpeak, or fit;
Deform'd in foul and every other part,
Affecting fight! enough to melt one's heart.

X.
Sometimes he laughs, and then a hideous yell,
That almoft equals the poor damn'd in hell;
When drown'd in drink we know not what we do,
We are defpifed and fcorn'd and cheated too.

XI.
On level with the beafts and far below
Are we when with ftrong drink we reeling go;
Below the devils when in this fin we run,
A drunken devil I never heard of one.

XII.
My kindred Indians, I intreat you all,
In this vile fin never again to fall;
Fly to the blood of CHRIST, for that alone
Can for this fin and all your fins atone.

XIII.
Though Mofes Paul is here alive and well,
This night his foul muft be in heaven or hell;
O! do take warning by this awful fight,
And to a JESUS make a fpeedy flight!

XIV.
You have no leafe of your fhort time you know,
To hell this night you may be forc'd to go;
Oh! do embrace an offer'd CHRIST to-day,
And get a fealed pardon while you may.

XV.
Behold a loving JESUS, fee him cry,
With earneftnefs of foul, "Why will ye die?"
My kindred Indians, come juft as you be,
Then Chrift and his falvation you fhall fee.

XVI.
If you go on and ftill reject Chrift's call,
'Twill be too late, his curfe will on you fall;
The Judge will doom you to that dreadful place,
In hell, where you fhall never fee his face.

Samson Occom, wrote this address in verse in 1772 at the execution of Moses Paul, an Indian. The address proselytizes for Christianity and condemns alcohol consumption by Indians. Traders encouraged Indians to indulge in alcohol while missionaries used the Indian susceptibility to it as proof of their depravity.

One verse reads, **"Our little children hovering round us weep, / Most starved to death we've nought for them to eat, / All this distress is justly on us come, / For the accursed use we make of rum."** Courtesy, American Antiquarian Society.

WilliamApess (Apes) was born a member of the Pequot tribe in 1798. Abandoned by his parents, he experienced considerable physical abuse at the hands of his alcoholic grandparents and was from age six "bound out" (indentured) to a series of white families where he encountered a mixture of continued abuse and religious instruction. Apess developed a love for alcohol that threatened to take his young life, but he experienced a religious conversion and a calling into the ministry (Haynes, 1996). Giving up liquor in 1824, Apess became known as the "Indian Preacher," and was ordained as a Methodist Minister in 1829--the same year he published the first widely read Native American biography, *A Son of the Forest* (McQuaid, 1977).

Apess' portrayal of brutality at the hands of his alcoholic grandparents, and accounts of his own drinking misadventures, stand as one of the earliest biographical depictions of alcoholism in American literature. He condemned alcohol as "the burning curse" and the "demon of despair," and was one of the first writers to speak directly to the children about the drinking of their parents:

> *Little children, if you have parents that drink the fiery waters, do all you can, both by your tears and prayers and friendly admonitions, to persuade them to stop; for it will most certainly ruin them, if they persist in it* (Apess, 1833, p. 125).

The sobered Apess pursued a somewhat conventional career as a Christian preacher with the Mashpee Indians until 1833. It was in this year that he came to view Christ as the savior of oppressed people and began to define his sobriety and his salvation within the devastating changes facing Indian tribes in the 1830s. Pursuing what would later be christened "liberation theology," Apess became a tireless organizer and campaigner for Mashpee political and economic rights. Anticipating Martin Luther King, Jr. by more than a century, Apess was branded an outside agitator in the white press and jailed for assault and inciting a riot in an incident in which

Apess refused to allow white men to cut and remove wood from tribal land. In a stunning act of civil disobedience, Apess sought his own arrest:

> *The fact is I was in no wise unwilling to go with him [the sheriff], or to have my conduct brought to the test of investigation...* (Quoted in Nielsen, 1985).

He did not waver in his condemnation of the treatment of Indian People--characterizing their treatment by whites as "one continued system of robbery." He also charged that the silence of Christian preachers had contributed to the "slavery and degradation" of Indians and Africans in America (McQuaid, 1977). Apess is one of the first Native writers that conceived a pan-Indian, intertribal, rather than a strictly tribal identity and portrayed peoples of color locked in a joint struggle for rights being taken from them by whites (Murray, 1991).

Through Apess' organizing efforts, the Mashpee won the right to self-incorporate and a degree of freedom to manage their own educational, economic and political affairs. This was, in fact, one of the few success stories during a period in which most Eastern Indian tribes experienced forced relocation west of the Mississippi and the growing paternalism of both federal and state governments. Kim McQuaid, author of a definitive account of Apess' life, comments on Apess' legacy:

> *New England Indians, however, did not disappear from the social and cultural scene. This fact is not an historic accident. Instead, it is due, in large part, to the efforts of little-known reformers like William Apes: crusaders for human dignity in a period when the future of the Indian within American society seemed nonexistent (McQuaid, 1977, p. 625).*

Throughout his years of activism, Apess viewed sobriety as a key to Native self-determination. He organized a Native temperance organization among the Mashpee and in his petition to the Governor of Massachusetts confronted the way Native appeals for justice were discounted because they were branded "poor drunken Indians." Apess' petition claimed that the Mashpee "have joined the temperance cause and wish to be counted so and heard..." (Nielsen, 1985).

These Nativist Christian movements were precursors of the wide spread of fundamentalist Christian sects among Native peoples--such as the Baptists and Seventh Day Adventists--all of whom required abstinence from alcohol as an article of faith. While many Native People were drawn to Christianity in the 18th and early 19th centuries, others accused the Christian preachers of trying to "tame" Indians so that they would be easier to kill (Wallace, 1956).

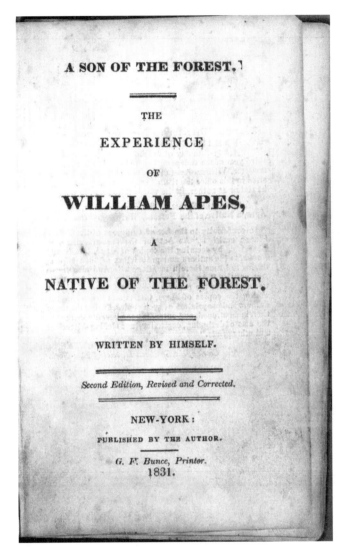

A SON OF THE FOREST.

THE

EXPERIENCE

OF

WILLIAM APES,

A

NATIVE OF THE FOREST.

WRITTEN BY HIMSELF.

Second Edition, Revised and Corrected.

NEW-YORK:

PUBLISHED BY THE AUTHOR.

G. F. Bunce, Printer.
1831.

A Son of the Forest is acknowledged to be the first published autobiography written by an American Indian. It tells the story of a life of abuse and oppression for a world of white readers in which Indians existed only as stereotypes. Apess had a Christian conversion experience in 1813 and preached as a Methodist, gradually rediscovering his cultural roots at a time when both Methodism and a Native American identity were generally scorned. Starting with *A Son of the Forest,* he spoke out against racism and ill treatment of Native People for the rest of his life.
Courtesy, Pocumtuck Valley Memorial Association, Deerfield MA.

References

Apess, W. (1833) *The Experiences of Five Christian Indians of the Pequot Tribe.* Published by the author.

Edwards, J. (1741). Sinners in the Hands of an Angry God. Sermon Delivered in Enfield, Connecticut, July 8, 1741. http://www.ccel.org/e/edwards/sermons/sinners.html Accessed September 11, 2005.

Haynes, C. (1996) "mark for them all to...hiss at": The formation of Methodist and Pequot identity in the conversion narrative of William Apess. *Early American Literature, 31*(1):25-44).

Love, W.D. (2000) *Samson Occom and the Christian Indians of New England.* Syracuse: Syracuse University Press.

McQuaid, K. (1977) William Apess, Pequot: An Indian reformer in the Jackson Era. *The New England Quarterly, 50*:605-625.

Murray, D. (1991) *Forked Tongue: Speech Writing and Representation in North American Indian Texts.* Bloomington, IN: Indiana University Press.

Nielsen, D. (1985) The Mashpee Indian Revolt of 1833. *The New England Quarterly, 58*:400-420.

Peyer, B. (1982) Samson Occom: Mohegan missionary and writer of the 18th century. *American Indian Quarterly, 6*(3,4 Fall/Winter):208-17.

Szasz, M.C. (1994) Samson Occom: Mohegan as spiritual intermediary. In: M.C.Szasz *Between Indian and White Worlds: The Cultural Broker.* Norman, OK: University of Oklahoma Press.

Thomas, R.K. (1981) The history of Native American Indian alcohol use as a community-based phenomenon. In Heath, D.B.; Waddell, J.O.; and Topper, M.D., Eds. *Cultural Factors in Alcohol Research and Treatment of Drinking Problems. Journal of Studies on Alcohol Supplement,* 929-39.

Chapter Eight

Handsome Lake Movement

Ganioda'yo (Ga-ne-odi-yo, Ganiodaio, Geneodiyo, Handsome Lake, Handsomlake) was born in 1735 within the Turtle clan of the Seneca tribe in the village of Ga-no-wau-ges (Canawaugus) on the Genesee River near what is today Avon, New York. The Senecas were part of the Confederacy known as the Iroquois, and Handsome Lake was one of forty-nine chiefs who sat on the council of the Confederacy.

During the Revolutionary War, Handsome Lake fought on the side of the British. He and his family were driven into a nomadic existence following Sullivan and his army's 1779 raid on Iroquois villages. Handsome Lake showed little leadership aptitude during his mid-life but was well-known because of the fame of his brother, Cornplanter, the great Seneca chief. In his sixties and suffering from alcoholism and a "wasting disease" (possibly recovery from delirium tremens), Handsome Lake, now little more than "yellow skin and dried bones," spent his days awaiting death, lamenting his years of drunkenness and the sorrows of his life (Wallace, 1969, p. 234, 240).

Cornplanter, Seneca, (1736-1836) was the brother of Handsome Lake. Handsome Lake lived at Cornplanter's land grant at the time he went through his recovery from alcohol and experienced the vision of the Messengers in 1799. Painting by F. Bartoli, Courtesy, Library of Congress

On June 15, 1799, now sixty-five and suffering from a several-week "bout with trade whiskey," Handsome Lake was thought to have died. After lying cold and breathless for seven hours, he suddenly awoke to pass on exhortations from the Great Spirit who had visited him in his death and who had sent him back with a message to Indian people. From this event until his death sixteen years later, Handsome Lake abstained from alcohol and became known as a great prophet who introduced a new and influential religion to the Iroquois. His new religion offered a beacon of hope at a time of heightened demoralization of the Iroquois due to a weakening of the Six Nations Confederacy (a league of the Cayuga, Mohawk, Oneida, Onondaga, Seneca, and Tuscarora), military defeat, the loss of tribal lands, encroachment of white settlers, loss of game, disease and poverty (Wallace, 1952).

The foundation of this new religion was the Gai'wiiò (Good Message), later known as the Code of Handsome Lake or the Longhouse Religion. The Code was described by anthropologist

Anthony Wallace as a "way of living and feeling...that plays an important part in the emotional lives" of those who adhere to it (Wallace, 1952, p. 150). The written Code was passed on in oral tradition until it was first written in the 1840s and later translated and published by Arthur Parker in 1913. The introduction of the Gai'wiiò describes how white men offered the Indian a "secret poison" that consumed the "elements of life," led to their exploitation ("bartering land for baubles") and personal destruction ("eats the life from their blood and crumbles their bones"). Handsome Lake depicted the effects of alcohol poisoning as a sickness (Parker, 1913, p. 18, 54-55):

And now furthermore a man becomes sick. Some strong power holds him...Now it comes to his mind that perchance evil has arisen because of strong drink and he resolves to use it nevermore. Now he continually thinks of this every day and every hour. Yea, he continually thinks of this. Then a time comes and he craves drink again for he thinks that he can not recover his strength without it. Now two ways he thinks: what once he did and whether he will ever recover (Parker, 1913, p. 19).

Handsome Lake (1735-1815) lay in his bed in recovery for four years. At the end of that time he had a vision in which three messengers came to him and brought many teachings about how the people should live, as well as many prophecies for the future. His extensive vision led to the Code of Handsome and the Longhouse Religion, which is still strong today.
(Drawing by contemporary artist Randell Hill, courtesy of the Jake Thomas Learning Centre)

The three messengers (right) took Handsome Lake along the sky road to view the world below and to see the future. As he looked back on Earth, many scenes of the future were revealed.
(Drawing by contemporary artist Randell Hill, courtesy of the Jake Thomas Learning Centre)

A fourth messenger joined Handsome Lake and the three messengers on his visit to the Land of the Creator, where many prophecies and truths were revealed.
(Drawing by contemporary artist Randell Hill, courtesy of the Jake Thomas Learning Centre)

The Gai'wiiò--Code of Handsome Lake--set forth its moral teachings in 128 Sections made up of brief exhortations and stories (Thomas, 1994). The centerpiece of the Code declared the following:

> *Four words tell a great story of wrong and the Creator is sad because of the trouble they bring, so go and tell your people. The first word is One'ga? [Whiskey or Rum]. It seems that you never have known that this word stands for a great and monstrous evil and has reared a high mound of bones...you lose your minds and one'ga? causes it all. Alas, many are...too fond of it. So now all must now say, "I will use it nevermore. As long as I live, as long as the number of my days is I will never use it again. I now stop" (Parker, 1913, p. 28).*

Handsome Lake also called for sobriety on behalf of children. Like Apess before him, he expressed great concern about the effect of parental drunkenness on children:

> *Tell your people that the Creator is sad because of what they are doing. Some people live together well as man and wife and family, but the man of the family uses strong drink. Then when he comes home he lifts up his child to fondle it and he is drunk. Now we, the messengers of the Creator, say that this is not right for if a man filled with strong drink touches his child he burns its blood. Tell your people to heed this warning (Parker, 1913, p. 35).*

When Handsome Lake revealed his vision to the tribal council, he spoke at length about drunkenness and its effects on Native People:

*You create a great sin in taking the firewater. The Great
Spirit says you must abandon this enticing habit. Your
ancestors have brought great misery upon you. They took
the firewater of the white man, and entailed upon you its
consequences. None of them have gone to heaven. The
firewater does not belong to you. It was made by the white
man beyond the great waters...The Great Spirit says
drunkenness is a great crime, and He forbids you to indulge
in this evil habit. His command is to the old and young. The
abandonment of its use will relieve much of your sufferings,
and greatly increase the comforts and happiness of your
children* (Quoted in Johnson, 1881, p. 192).

The Gai'wiiò threatened those who adored the "fiery drink" on
earth with images of an afterlife in which the Punisher would pour
molten metal down their throats (Parker, 1913, p. 71).

Those sections of the Gai'wiiò not addressing alcohol call for
Handsome Lake's followers to eschew other actions and traits (e.g.,
vainness, boasting, gossip, gambling, sexual promiscuity, and
violence towards women and children) while embracing others (e.g.,
living in community, caring for the elderly and the poor, and
generosity). Handsome Lake organized "circles" that met quarterly
and were run by a leader called a "holder" who was authorized to
preach and interpret the Gai'wiiò (Cherrington, 1925-26).

In the first decade of the nineteenth century, many observers
noted the marked sobriety of villages that had come under the
influence of Handsome Lake. In a letter sent to Handsome Lake in
1803, Thomas Jefferson commended him for recognizing the
"ruinous effects" of alcohol on Native People and for calling for its
complete rejection (please see Appendix 1 in this book). Reports this
same year from Cornplanter's sister note that the Seneca had kept
faith with their resolve "to drink it [alcohol] no more." Traders in
Pittsburgh were forced to substitute sugar-water for refreshment
because the Seneca refused to drink their whiskey (Deardorff, 1951).

Elias Johnson's nineteenth century history of the Six Nations describes the effect of Handsome Lake's teachings as follows: "Many abandoned their dissolute habits and became sober, moral men; discord and contentions gave place to harmony and order, and vagrancy and sloth to ambition and industry" (Johnson, 1881, p. 187).

Handsome Lake's influence extended long after his death in 1815, particularly through the continued teaching of his grandson, Sos=he:owâ (Sosheowa, Sase-ha-wa) (Parker, 1913). Between 1818 and 1845, the Handsome Lake Religion was formally organized into a church whose mission was the propagation of the teachings of Handsome Lake (Wallace, 1969). The Longhouse Religion continues today, confirming the prophesy of Handsome Lake that "Gai'wiiò is only in its beginning" (Wallace, 1969).

Handsome Lake was followed by other Iroquois prophets who preached abstinence-based religions and continued Handsome Lake's practice of organizing temperance/recovery circles. This network of recovery circles evolved in the 1830s into the Six Nations Temperance League (Johnson, 1881).

Chief Jacob Thomas, Cayuga, (1922-1998) holder of the Handsome Lake Teachings, and a Faithkeeper of the Longhouse Religion is pictured outside a traditional Longhouse. Chief Thomas, with the assistance of Terry Boyle wrote a book called Teachings From the Longhouse published in 1994. Teachings From the Longhouse is the Code of Handsome Lake as expressed by Elder-practitioner in the early 1990's and is the most recent expression in writing of the Code since Parker and Wallace.
(Photo courtesy of Jake Thomas Learning Centre)

References

Cherrington, E. (1925-1926) Ed. *Standard Encyclopedia of the Alcohol Problem,* (Six Volumes). Westerville, Ohio, American Issue Publishing Company.

Deardorff, M.H. (1951) The religion of Handsome Lake: Its origin and development. Symposium on Local Diversity in Iroquois Culture, ed., W.N. Fenton, *Bureau of American Ethnology, Bulletin,* 149:77-107.

Johnson, E. (1881) *Legends, Traditions and Laws of the Iroquois or Six Nations.* Lockport, NY: Union Printing and Publishing Company.

Parker, A.C. (1913) *The Code of Handsome Lake.* New York State Museum Bulletin 163:70-74.

Thomas, Chief Jacob (1994) *Teachings from the Longhouse.* With Terry Boyle. Toronto, Ontario, Canada: Stoddart Publishing Co. Limited

Wallace, A. (1952) Handsome Lake and the great revival in the west. *American Quarterly, 4*(2):149-165.

Wallace, A. (1969) *The Death and Rebirth of the Seneca.* New York: Vintage Books.

A contemporary traditional Six Nations (Iroquois or Haudenesaunee) longhouse constructed of traditional materials (left), and a temporary design made of canvas in use today (right).

Chapter Nine

The Prophets
American Indian Prophets, Temperance Societies and the Indian Shaker Church

Tenskwatawa, the Shawnee Prophet

Like the Iroquois, the Shawnee opened the nineteenth century confronted with white encroachment, rampant disease, and a growing problem of alcoholism, described at the time as "a passion for drink that knows no bounds" (Edmunds, 1983, p. 23). Hope and leadership came from two men fathered by the Shawnee chief, Puckeshinewa. His sons were Tecumseh, the great political leader, and Tenskwatawa, who brought sobriety and a new religion to the Shawnee. Born in 1775 in a Shawnee village along the Mad River in Ohio, Tenskwatawa (known in childhood as Lalawetheke or Elkswatawa) had, like his brother Tecumseh, developed a taste for the "white man's firewater."

Tenskwatawa was known as a drunkard and a braggart and had little status within his tribe. His attempt to replace Penagasha, a respected medicine man, was met with skepticism from tribal members who wondered how one so wounded himself could still heal others (Edmunds, 1983).

In April, 1805, Tenskwatawa was thought to have died, and preparations of his body had begun for the burial ritual. Those assembled with his wife were thus stunned to see him awake from this non-breathing state and report that he had been sent back from death with messages from the Master of Life. Declaring that he would henceforth be known as Tenskwatawa--Open Door--he detailed a vision of the future destruction of Indian People if they followed the white man's drinking practices. Weeping for himself and his tribe, he vowed to never again drink whiskey (Cherrington, 1925-26; Edmunds, 1983).

Becoming widely known as the Shawnee Prophet, Tenskwatawa launched a total abstinence campaign that for several years reduced alcohol problems among the Shawnee as well as the Wyandot, Creek, Choctaw, Sauk, Fox, Winnebago, Arikara, Ottawa, Chippewas, Assiniboins, Sioux, Mandan and Blackfoot. Tenskwatawa, like Handsome Lake, encased the call for sobriety within a larger moral code. This code condemned promiscuity, polygamy, intertribal violence, and accumulation of personal wealth. It reaffirmed the virtues of marital fidelity; respect for wives, children and elders; and communal sharing, all of which were traditional (Hirshfelder and Molin, 2001). New ceremonies were developed that included ritual confession and "shaking hands with the Prophet," a ritual in which converts solemnly drew strings of beads through their hands--a ritual visually akin to saying the Catholic rosary (Edmunds, 1983).

The Shawnee Prophet also called for disengagement from whites, going so far as prohibiting trade with whites and calling upon Indian women who had married white men to return to their tribes, leaving their children with their white fathers. His refusal to recognize the legality of treaties, his threats to kill the chiefs who had signed away tribal lands, and his promise to not allow settlers into ceded tribal lands brought increasing conflict and the Prophet's subsequent exile to Canada.

Two Shawnee Brothers

Tenskwatawa

Tenskwatawa recovered from his own alcohol problems, going on to champion abstinence and a return to the culture from an orientation of culture and spirituality. In 1808 he said, *"I told the red skins that the way they were in was not good, and they ought to abandon it; that we should consider ourselves as one man, that we ought to live agreeable to our several customs–the red man after their mode, and the white people after theirs; particularly, they should not drink whiskey; that it was not made for them, and that it is the cause of all the mischiefs the Indians suffer"* (Armstrong, 1971, p.43).

Photo courtesy, McKenney-Hall Portrait Gallery of American Indians.

Tecumseh

Tecumseh also recovered from alcohol use and dedicated his life to a return to the culture from more of a political viewpoint. He worked tirelessly to unite many tribes in a confederacy but was not successful. In 1811 he voiced his famous "Never, never" speech when he said, *"Where today are the Pequot? Where are the Narragansett, the Mohican, the Pokanoket, and many other once powerful tribes of our people? They have vanished before the avarice and the oppression of the White Man, as snow before a summer sun. Will we let ourselves be destroyed in our turn without a struggle, give up our homes, our country bequeathed to us by the Great Spirit, the graves of our dead and everything that is dear and sacred to us? I know you will cry with me, 'Never! Never!'"* (Brown, 1972, p.1) He voiced his opposition to alcohol with the words, *"Touch not the poisonous firewater that makes wise men turn to fools and robs the spirit of its vision"* (Lombardi, 1982, p.34).

Photo courtesy Library of Congress

Tenskwatawa argued for sobriety as a strategy that would not only provide personal and community renewal, but also provide a defensive shield that would lessen the ability of whites to victimize Indian People (Lender, 1984, p. 482). His admonition not to drink was so effective that Indian traders in Michigan complained that they could not sell a gallon of whiskey in a month (Dowd, 1992b)--a fact confirmed by reports from James Mooney on the sobriety of those tribes in the Central West who had heard the Prophet's message (Cherrington, 1925-26). Referring to the effect of Tenskwatawa's teachings, Mooney reported that "Those who were addicted to drunkenness...were so thoroughly alarmed at the prospects of fiery punishment in the spirit-world that, for a long time, intoxication became practically unknown among the western tribes" (Quoted in Johnson, 1911, p. 183).

The influence of Tenskwatawa declined following the Battle of Tippecanoe and his ten-year exile to Canada. Eventually returning to the United States, The Shawnee Prophet died in November 1836.

Kennekuk, the Kickapoo Prophet

Kennekuk (Kannekuk, Keeanakik, Putting His Foot Down, Pakaka, Pah-kah-kah, the Kickapoo Prophet) emerged in the 1830s as a religious and political leader of the Kickapoo and Pottawatomie tribes. He was widely recognized for his intelligence (he spoke six languages), his charisma and eloquence, and his political insight. Rather than completely rejecting the customs and beliefs of whites, Kennekuk created a unique mixture of Christian (Methodism and Roman Catholicism) and Native beliefs, the centerpiece of which was the complete rejection of alcohol (Hirshfelder and Molin, 2001).

Kennekuk's repeated criticism of liquor as a tool of personal and cultural injury was reinforced by physical surveillance, confiscation, and destruction of liquor brought into tribal land (Schultz, 1980). R. Baldwin, the agent of the Kickapoo tribe, noted in 1856 that enduring temperance followed Kennekuk's campaign against alcohol. He reported that "many Indians who had been in the habit of drinking this liquor vastly to excess had decided to abandon its use entirely" (Frederikson, 1932 p. 67).

Kennekuk's rejection of alcohol emerged out of both personal and cultural experiences. Known early in his life as the "Drunkard's Son" (a reference to his father's alcoholism), Kennekuk himself became known as "a bad young man, a drunkard." While in a drunken rage, he killed his uncle and, as a result, was rejected by his own people for a period (Herring, 1988). Having been personally wounded by the white man's "wicked water," Kennekuk saw with heightened clarity the larger devastation that alcohol was inflicting on individual Indians, families and tribes (Schultz, 1980, Unrau, 1996, p. 23).

Widely known as the Kickapoo Prophet, Kennekuk introduced an abstinence-based religion that uniquely combined many elements of religious practice: the use of town criers to call people to prayer, the use of prayer sticks with carved characters that guided chanting and singing, and a moral code that prohibited lying, profanity, and stealing as well as drunkenness. Kennekuk also introduced the use of ritualized public confession and whipping to make amends for guilt and strengthen moral discipline. It was a common practice for those so punished to thank those inflicting the punishment for relieving them of the burden of sin. Christian missionaries condemned Kennekuk's teachings, and white politicians recognized him as a formidable opponent as he championed the rights of Native tribes (Herring, 1988).

In his later years, Kennekuk referred to himself as the Son of God who had been sent to the Indians as Jesus had been sent to the Whites (Schultz, 1980). The religion of Kennekuk provided a framework of both prevention and recovery among the Kickapoo and Pottawatomie during the mid-nineteenth century. Following the Prophet's death in 1852 from smallpox, these tribes, who had already experienced multiple relocations, saw their tribal lands shrink from the initial reserve of 768,000 acres to a paltry six square miles. In the face of such devastation, Kennekuk's teachings continued to be passed on by his successor, Wansuck, who had committed the Prophet's teaching to writing (Custer, 1918).

Indian Temperance Societies and Missionaries

Many Native tribes responded to the calls of their leaders to reject alcohol by organizing their own temperance societies. By 1836, several tribes (Otoes, Kanzas, Cherokees, and Osages) had organized temperance societies. The Cherokees began agitation against alcohol in 1829 and by 1836 had organized the Cherokee Temperance Society. The Cherokee, who were about to begin the infamous "trail of tears" in the winter of 1838-1839, characterized alcohol as a dangerous enemy in the preamble to their signed pledge:

> *A powerful enemy is abroad in our country...The mourning of the widow and the orphan is heard wherever that enemy has been...Let us arise, and put him to death, or banish him beyond the limits of the Cherokee Nation* (Cherrington, 1925-26, p. 25).

Such sentiments were not limited to the Cherokee. The Shawnee tribal councilor, Blackhoof, declared in the 1830s:

> *I myself saw the evils of drinking whiskey ten years ago, and I quit drinking, and I have prospered ever since...My friends, this is the course we had better all pursue in the future...*

An 1851 report from Kansas noted that nearly all members of the Weas, Piankeshaws, Peorias, and Kaskaskias had signed a pledge of abstinence and that the habit of sobriety was becoming entrenched within these tribes (Frederikson, 1932). The Ottawas organized their own temperance society in 1839, and Native temperance societies and pledge signing were commonplace in the 1840s and 1850s (Unrau, 1996).

The spread of these societies was facilitated by Native temperance missionaries like Kahgegagahbowh, also known as George Copway. Kahgegagahbowh (Ojibwa) was born in 1818 and raised in Ontario. Both he and his father recovered from alcoholism through the medium of religious conversion, the son in 1830 just before his mother's death. Kahgegagahbowh became a well-known temperance missionary and preacher offering an apocalyptic message of how alcohol (the "devil's spittle") would make Indian People "fade away like frost before the heat of the sun" (Cherrington, 1925-26, p. 21; Ruoff, 1987). Copway said,

> *Poor untutored red men! You were deluded, and made drunk by white men, and then in your hellish drunken passions, you turn around and imbrued your hands in the blood of your own relatives and brethren* (Copway, 1847, 1997, p. 83).

Kahgegagahbowh's message focused on the redemptive power of religious conversion and sobriety, the effects of which were well-articulated by a Chippewa chief in 1839:

> *Before I heard the gospel, I began to thank the Great Spirit for the day on which I could get plenty of whiskey. Brothers, you know how often I was dragged through the snow to my wigwam, where my wife and children were cold and hungry. Now, I drink tea instead of whiskey, and have religion with it; now my house is comfortable; and my children are pious and happy* (Quoted in Copway, 1847, 1997, p. 127).

George Copway, (Kahgegagahbowh or Stands Fast), Ojibwa (1818-1869) recovered from alcoholism, becoming a well-known Ojibwa temperance reformer in the early 1800's

Copway's missionary and temperance work, which was conducted in Canada and the United States (particularly in Minnesota), often brought him into conflict with white authorities. He rejected any hint of subordinate status among his religious peers and braved criticism following his marriage to the daughter of an English settler in 1833 (Smith, 1988).

Even Native leaders who continued to struggle with their own alcoholism tried to influence others toward temperance. Bib Legs, the principal chief of the Miamis in the 1850s, suffered from habitual drunkenness but continued to regularly warn young men of the tribe about the evils of intemperance (Frederikson, 1932).

In the late 1800s, and into the early 20th century, abstinence-based temperance and mutual aid societies emerged among several Native Alaskan tribes. These included the Indian Mutual Aid Society and the Alaskan Native Brotherhood (Andersen, 1988).

THE

LIFE, HISTORY, AND TRAVELS,

OF

KAH-GE-GA-GAH-BOWH

(GEORGE COPWAY),

A YOUNG INDIAN CHIEF OF THE OJEBWA NATION,

A CONVERT TO THE CHRISTIAN FAITH, AND A MISSIONARY
TO HIS PEOPLE FOR TWELVE YEARS;

WITH A

SKETCH OF THE PRESENT STATE OF THE OJEBWA NATION,

IN REGARD TO

CHRISTIANITY AND THEIR FUTURE PROSPECTS.

ALSO AN APPEAL;

WITH ALL THE NAMES OF THE CHIEFS NOW LIVING, WHO HAVE
BEEN CHRISTIANIZED, AND THE MISSIONARIES NOW
LABORING AMONG THEM.

WRITTEN BY HIMSELF.

ALBANY :
PRINTED BY WEED AND PARSONS.
1847.

George Copway, from the Mississauga Band of the Ojibwe, was an author whose autobiographical works were some of the earliest published writings by a Native American. He wrote seven books from 1847 to 1858, *The Life, History and Travels...* being the first.
Courtesy, Native American Authors Project

Squ-sacht-un (John Slocum) and the Indian Shaker Church

The Indian Shaker Church was founded in 1882 by Squ-sacht-un (John Slocum) and his wife Whe-bul-eht-sah (Mary Thompson) of the Sahewamish tribe. Slocum was a self-described "bad Indian" who had wasted most of his life drinking and gambling. In November, 1882, Slocum died (or was thought to have died) near Olympia Washington. During the wake, Slocum awoke to report a most remarkable experience. He reported having died and, after seeing a great "shining light" (not unlike that later described by A.A. co-founder Bill Wilson), was told by an angel of God that Slocum and his people should live as Christian Indians. The angel promised salvation to Native People if they would forsake alcohol, tobacco, and gambling and live a Christian life. The angel offered Slocum the chance to live again if he would deliver this message to Indian People and live a sober, moral life (Lehnoff, 1982).

The Shaker religion emerged at a time of rapid infusion of white settlers into Native lands of the Northwest. Within six years (1880-1886), the white population had swelled from 75,000 to 210,000 (Smith, 1954). For the Native tribes of the Northwest, it was a time of great loss and disillusionment, a time of great need (Collins, 1950).

The religion that emerged from Slocum's experience blended elements of Protestant theology and morality with elements of Native traditional beliefs and ceremonies. It was Slocum's wife, Mary, who introduced the bodily shake from which the Shaker Church would draw its name. The use of the shake as a healing ritual was portrayed as having special properties as an agent of healing and as a spiritual alternative to drunkenness. Missionary Helen Clark, having observed that those Indians who shook lost their desire for alcohol, concluded that shaking (Shakerism) was an alternative to staggering (alcoholism) (Ruby and Brown, 1996).

The Indian Shaker Church called for sobriety mixed with a blend of Euro-American and Native religious traditions. It filled a void at a time that Native communities in the Northwest were suffering from a loss of traditions, growing poverty and widespread alcoholism. It was a time period that Indian people called "the end of the world" and "the end of Indian time." The first church was built on the Squaxin Island Indian Reservation in South Puget Sound. The sobriety-based Indian Shaker Church was presented not as a new religion but as a return to Native traditions (Buckley, 1997). Early accounts note the role of this new religion in rescuing many Native People from the curse of alcoholism (Brown, 1910). The Indian Shaker Church has continued to be acknowledged by alcoholism experts as having served as a viable sobriety-based support structure for many Native American alcoholics (Slagle and Weibel-Orlando, 1986). Like the Code of Handsome Lake, the Indian Shaker Church called upon Native People to give up drinking; stop lying, stealing, and gambling; and to live a moral life.

References

Anderson, T.I. (1988). *Alaska Hooch.* Fairbanks, AK: Hoo-Che-Noo.

Armstrong, V. (1971). *I have Spoken: American History Through the Voices of the Indians.* Chicago, Il: Swallow Press

Brown, D. (1910). *Indian Workers for Temperance. Collier's,* September 3, pp. 23-24.

Brown, D. (1972). *Bury My Heart at Wounded Knee.* New York, Bantam Books

Buckley, T. (1997). The Shaker Chruch and the Indian Way in Native Northwestern California. *The American Indian Quarterly, 21*(1):1-14.

Cherrington, E., Ed. (1925-1926). *Standard Encyclopedia of the Alcohol Problem,* (Six Volumes). Westerville, Ohio, American Issue Publishing Company.

Collins, J. (1950). The Indian Shaker Church. *Southwestern Journal of Anthropology, 6:*403-412.

Copway, G. (1847). *The Life, History and Travels of Kah-Ge=Ga-Gah-Bowh (George Copway) A Young Indian Chief of the Ojebwa Nation.* Philadelphia: James Hamstead.   Reprinted as   Copway, G. (Kahgegagahbowh)(1997) *Life, Letters, and Speeches.* Eds. A. LaVonne Brown Ruoff and Donald B. Smith. Lincoln: University of Nebraska Press.

Custer, M. (1918). Kannekuk or Keeanakuk, the Kickapoo Prophet. *Journal of the Illinois Historical Society, 5*(11, April), pp. 48-56

Dowd, G.E. (1992b). Thinking and believing: Nativism in the age of Pontiac and Tecumseh. *American Indian Quarterly, 16*(3):309-335.

Edmunds, R.D. (1983). *The Shawnee Prophet.* Lincoln: University of Nebraska Press.

Frederikson, O. (1932). *The Liquor Question Among the Indian Tribes in Kansas: 1804-1881.* Lawrence, KA: University of Kansas.

Herring, J.B. (1988). *Kenekuk, the Kickapoo Prophet,* Lawrence, KA: University of Kansas Press.

Hirschfelder, A. and Molin, P. (2001). *Encyclopedia of Native American Religion.* New York: Checkmark Books.

Johnson, W.E. (1911). *The Federal Government and the Liquor Traffic.* Westerville, Ohio: The American Issue Publishing Company.

Lehnoff, P. (1982). Indian Shaker Religion. *American Indian Quarterly, 6*(Fall and Winter):283-290.

Lender, M. (1984). *Dictionary of American Temperance Biography.* Westport, Connecticut: Greenwood Press.

Lombardi, F.G. (1982). *Circle Without End.* Happy Camp, CA: Naturegraph

Ruby, R. and Brown, J. (1996). *John Slocum and the Indian Shaker Church.* Norman: University of Oklahoma.

Ruoff, A.L.B. (1987). George Copway: Nineteenth century American Indian autobiographer. *Auto-Biography, 3*(2):6-17.

Schultz, G. (1980). *Kennekuk: The Kickapoo Prophet.* Topeka, KS: Kansas State Historical Society.

Slagle, L. and Weibel-Orlando, J. (1986). The Indian Shaker Church and Alcoholics Anonymous Revitalistic Curing Cults. *Human Organization, 45*(4):310-319.

Smith, D. (1988). The life of George Copway or Kah-ge-ga-gah-bowh (1818-1869) and a review of his writings. *Journal of Canadian Studies, 23*(2):5-38.

Smith, M.W. (1954). Shamanism in the Shaker religion of the northwest America. *Man, LIV*:119-22.

Unrau, William (1996). *White Man's Wicked Water: The Alcohol Trade and Prohibition in Indian Country, 1802-1892.* Lawrence, KA: University Press of Kansas.

Chapter Ten

Peyote, the Native American Church and Recovery from Alcoholism

Before I joined the peyote I went about in a most pitiable condition, and now I am living happily and my wife has a fine baby.

—Crashing Thunder, Winnebago, 1909

The Mescalero Apaches and other Southwestern tribes were exposed to peyote in their travels to Mexico and incorporated the ritual use of peyote into their own tribal customs as early as 1760 (Rudgley, 1994). Peyote was regarded as a "vegetable incarnation of a deity" and careful rules were laid out for its respectful use within the framework of religious ritual (Shultes, 1972). Peyotism, as practiced by organized Sacred Peyote Societies, spread rapidly in the 1870s and 1880s from the Apaches to the Omahas, Kiowas, and Comanches, eventually reaching Native tribes all the way into Canada. The diffusion of the peyote ritual occurred as Southwestern tribes were coming under physical and cultural assault, and Eastern tribes were being forced further and further west into "Indian

Territory." The central figure in the rise of Peyotism was Zuanah, or Quanah Parker, Comanche.

Quanah Parker (ca. 1845-1911), Quahadi Comanche, was influential in the spread of Christian peyotism among the Plains Indians in the 19th and early 20th centuries. Some of his work led to the founding of the Native American Church (NAC) in 1918.

Quanah Parker was born in May 1845, the son of Comanche chief Nocona (Nocone, Niconi), and Cynthia Ann Parker, a white woman who had grown up in the Comanche tribe since being captured when she was nine years old. As a child, he survived the loss of both of his parents and the subsequent death of the woman who adopted him. He survived his marginalization as a "mixed-blood," and he survived the dislocation and threatened starvation of his tribe (Jackson and Jackson, 1963; Hagan, 1993). Like so many Native leaders depicted in this book, he also survived his own encounters with alcohol. It is not surprising that the rejection of alcohol emerged as a centerpiece of the intertribal, peyote religion that Quanah Parker, John Rave, and other Native leaders spread throughout North America (La Barre, 1947, p. 298). Until his death in February, 1911, Parker played a prominent role in spreading the Peyote Way by conducting peyote meetings and defending the ritual use of peyote when it came under attack. Like Parker, John Rave had also been known as a heavy drinker before his involvement with peyote. In the meetings that he led, Rave attributed his own ability to stop drinking to the peyote medicine (Hertzberg 1971).

Reuben A. Snake Jr., Winnebago (Ho Chunk), (1937-1993), was a popular NAC Road Chief whose work led directly to passage of the 1994 Peyote amendment of the American Indian Religious Freedom Act of 1978.

Ritual Peyote use was first fully described in an anthropological study conducted by LaBarre published in 1938 as *The Peyote Cult*. Later studies by J.S. Slotkin in 1956 (*The Peyote Religion*) (Slotkin, 1956), and David Aberle in 1966 (*The Peyote Religion among the Navaho*) (Aberle, 1966), further detailed variations in the ritual use of peyote by Native People. The peyote ritual varies, with three major types of rituals or ceremonies described in the literature (Quintero, 1992). The early ritual combined the hallucinogenic effects of peyote with fasting, chanting, prayers of supplication and thanksgiving, sustained sleeplessness, and moral teaching. The early Peyote ceremony varied from tribe to tribe, but generally included the following elements. First came a period of preparation, which might include fasting, sexual abstinence, bathing, and the sweat lodge. Some participants painted their faces and bodies, using patterns and colors that represented their prior experience with peyote. Dress for the ceremony varied by tribe and geographical location. The ceremony took place at night, with participants sitting around a fire in a large tepee, or in an open space in front of a crescent-shaped altar. The ceremony was conducted by a "Road Chief," or "Road Man," who opened the ceremony by placing a large button--"Father Peyote"--in a groove on the altar. A Road Chief or Road Man is Native spiritual leader knowledgeable in the way of the Peyote Road. Participants chewed four to twelve peyote buttons and sometimes drank peyote tea. The night was spent chanting, singing "peyote songs," praying, interpreting visions, and passing ceremonial objects (LaBarre, 1974).

The early peyote ritual often included public confession, crying, and requests for pardon. Water-bringing ceremonies, used in healing rituals, took place at midnight and at dawn. In the morning, there were discussions of the visions and their meaning, teaching about the Peyote Way, and a communal breakfast for participants. The ritual included periods of silent introspection, prayers, chants and songs, drumming, and instruction (Pascarosa, Futterman, and Halsweig, 1976). A psychological description of the total experience might include such modern terms as "surrender" and "ego-death." The peyote ritual served to strengthen and deepen cultural identification and cohesion as Pascarosa and Futterman reveal:

> *The feeling of extended family is heightened by the practice of addressing old and dear friends as though they were blood relatives. Elders frequently refer to younger members as "son" or "nephew"; and an intimate friend becomes a "brother"* (Pascarosa and Futterman, 1976, p. 215).

A late 19th century peyote ceremony (left) and a contemporary 20th century NAC ceremony (right) are pictured here. Photo (left) courtesy of Smithsonian National Anthropological Archives.

The Peyote Way (Peyote Road; Tipi Way) is an ethical code of conduct that reflects the values that Peyotists strive to embrace. The Peyote Way demands care of family, brotherly love, generosity, self-reliance, and sobriety (Slotkin, 1956). The peyote ethic demanded faithfulness in marriage, fulfillment of kinship duties, hard work, and, most important for our story, abstinence from alcohol (LaBarre, 1974).

A Cheyenne Peyote
Church leader, ca 1922

Thomas Hill (Hill, 1990), documented the diffusion of the peyote religion among the Winnebago in the early 1900s, and the way in which its spread significantly reduced alcohol problems among members of the tribe. One of the first earliest and best first person accounts we have is in the autobiography of Crashing Thunder, a Winnebago Indian whose life story was recorded in 1909 and later published (Radin, 1926). This biography describes the transformation of Crashing Thunder from a self-described confirmed drunkard, thief, murderer and convict to a respected practitioner of the peyote religion. After converting to the peyote religion in 1889, Crashing Thunder reflected on his alcoholism:

> *Many years ago I had been sick and it looked as if this*
> *sickness were going to kill me. I tried all the Winnebago*
> *doctors and I tried all the white man's medicines, all were of*
> *no avail. I thought to myself, "You are doomed. I wonder*
> *whether you will be alive next year?" Such were the*
> *thoughts that came to me. As soon as I ate the peyote,*
> *however, I got over my sickness. After that I was not sick*
> *again.* (Radin, 1926, p. 182).

An incident that occurred during one of Crashing Thunder's first peyote experiences illustrates the potential emotional power of the peyote ritual.

> *After midnight I would every now and then hear someone*
> *cry. In some cases I saw a person go up to the leader and*
> *talk with him. I was told what these people were saying. I*
> *was told that these people were sorry for the sins they had*
> *committed and wished to be prevented from committing them*
> *again. They cried very loudly* (Radin, 1926, p. 177).

Almost fifty years later, articles would appear in psychiatric journals attesting to the utility of peyote in the treatment of alcoholism and noting the effectiveness of the Native American Church in reducing "feelings of alienation and isolation by allowing safe, cathartic expression of inner feelings" (Albaugh and Anderson, 1974, p. 1249).

Like sobriety-based support structures that appeared later in history, the Peyote Way made complete abstinence a socially legitimate choice and provided alternative rituals that met many of the same needs that people had previously met through drinking (Hill, 1990, p. 259). The role of peyote in reducing alcoholism was a prominent theme in testimony before Congress in opposition to a Bill that would have legally prohibited Indian peyote use. James Mooney, the first anthropologist to study Native peyote use, defended the practice on the grounds that "no real peyote user touches whiskey or continues to drink whiskey after he has taken up the peyote religion." He called peyote the Indian's "greatest shield against intemperance" (Quoted in Hertzberg, 1971, p. 266). Fred Lookout, Chief of the Osage, reported that among the Osage peyote had turned drunkards into citizens of good reputation (Hertzberg, 1971), and Alanson Skinner reported in 1915 that "the effect of peyote on the Kansa has been to abolish drunkenness among its followers" (Quoted in Hill, 1990, p. 255).

Participation in the Peyote religion proved so effective at reversing long-standing alcohol problems that some observers speculated that peyote might be pharmacologically incompatible with alcohol (Albaugh and Anderson, 1974; LaBarre, 1974). This proposition has since been discredited (Hill, 1990).

The Peyote Way's prescription for sobriety gave Native Americans a cultural pathway for abstinence from alcohol and opened up a method of treating Native alcoholism. Even those who lobbied against the availability of peyote often grudgingly admitted that many alcoholic Indians had stopped drinking through their participation in Peyotism (Hertzberg, 1971). Efforts at suppression led early followers of Peyotism to seek legal protection by formalizing their practices into an organized religion. Peyotism was incorporated into the First-Born Church of Christ, and then into the more enduring Native American Church of the United States, which was founded on October 10, 1918. The name was changed to Native American Church of North America in 1955, when Peyotism spread to Canada. The charter set forth the Church's aspirational values: "morality, sobriety, industry, kindly charity and right living and to cultivate a spirit of self-respect and brotherly union among members of the Native Race of Indians" (Quoted in Hertzberg, 1971, p. 273). Today, the Native American Church has grown to more than 250,000 Native people, involving more than 60 tribes from all over the United States and Canada (Schleiffer, 1973).

American Indian Religious Freedom Act Amendments of 1994
Public Law 103-344
108 Stat. 3124

Passed by 103rd Congress
Oct 6, 1994

[H.R. 4230]

An Act

To emend the American Indian Religious Freedom Act to provide for the traditional use of peyote by Indians for religious purposes, and for other purposes.

Be it enacted by the Senate and House of Representatives of the United States of America in Congress assembled,

SECTION 1. SHORT TITLE.

This Act may be cited as the "American Indian Religious Freedom Act Amendments of 1994".

SECTION 2. TRADITIONAL INDIAN RELIGIOUS USE OF THE PEYOTE SACRAMENT.

The Act of August 11, 1978 (42 U.S.C. 1996), commonly referred to as the "American Indian Religious Freedom Act", is amended by adding at the end thereof the following new section:

"SECTION 3.

a.   The Congress finds and declares that

1.   for many Indian people, the traditional ceremonial use of the peyote cactus as a religious sacrament has for centuries been integral to a way of life, and significant in perpetuating Indian tribes and cultures;

2.   since 1965, this ceremonial use of peyote by Indians has been protected by Federal regulation;

3.   while at least 28 States have enacted laws which are similar to, or are in conformance with, the Federal regulation which protects the ceremonial use of peyote by Indian religious practitioners, 22 States have not done so, and this lack of uniformity has created hardship for Indian people who participate in such religious ceremonies;

4.   the Supreme Court of the United States, in the case of Employment Division v. Smith, 494 U.S. 872 (1990), held that the First Amendment does not protect Indian practitioners who use peyote in Indian religious ceremonies, and also raised uncertainty whether this religious practice would be protected under the compelling State interest standard; and

5.the lack of adequate and clear legal protection for the religious use of peyote by Indians may serve to stigmatize and marginalize Indian tribes and cultures, and increase the risk that they will be exposed to discriminatory treatment.   CONTINUED...

American Indians received a guarantee by law for their use of the Peyote Sacrament by an Amendment to the American Indian Religious Freedom Act (1978) in 1994. Peyote buttons (*Lophophora williamsii*) are shown in the inset.

The Native American Church provided then and still today provides:

1) a new way to conceive alcohol, alcoholism, personal identity and one's purpose for living—what Quintero (Quintero, 1992, p. 92) calls an "epistemological shift,"

2) a culturally approved means of expressing strong emotion,

3) a means for restructuring family and social relationships,

4) an alternative sobriety-based support structure for recovering Indian people, and

5) a new value system (the Peyote Road).

Albaugh and Anderson (1974), Stewart (1987) and Quintero (1992) have interviewed many Native People for whom the peyote ceremony marked the turning point in their recovery from alcoholism. The potential role of the Native American Church and the peyote ritual in the treatment of alcoholism has also been noted by such respected psychiatrists as Dr. Karl Menninger. Menninger considered the peyote ritual a more effective remedy for Native alcoholism than any methods offered by the mainstream culture (LaBarre, 1975).

The recognition of the potential role of peyote in the treatment of Native alcoholism has continued the past few decades (Bergman, 1971; Albaugh and Anderson, 1974; Pascarosa and Futterman, 1976; Pascarosa, Futterman and Halsweig, 1976; Blum, Futterman and Pascarosa, et al, 1977). Garrity has described this role:

> *The distinct ability of both the NAC [Native American Church] and Pentecostal Christianity to provide new communities, new moralities, new forms of power, and new forms of control are significant therapeutic elements for individuals who suffer from alcohol and substance abuse problems...the NAC engagement of alcohol is characterized by themes of hope, transformation, new ways of living, and sense of power over alcohol (Garrity, 2000).*

In the Native American Church, one gains power over alcohol only after one has been healed by the "power of the medicine" (peyote).   When the Road Men of the Native American Church challenge the alcoholic to "ask the medicine," and "listen to what the medicine tells you," they are tapping deep recovery traditions that in contemporary language might be described as surrender, acceptance, self-inventory, confession and reaching powers lying within and outside oneself.   The peyotist, like his Alcoholics Anonymous counterpart, becomes part of a new social world and takes on new and fulfilling roles (e.g., singer, drummer, fireman, or cedarman) within the peyote ritual (Garrity, 2000).   The congregations of today's Native American Church have been described as "rich with recovered alcoholics" (Pascarosa, Futterman, and Halsweig, 1976, p. 518), and surveys of North American Indians in recovery from alcoholism often attribute their abstinence to participation in peyote rituals (Roy, et al, 1970; Roy, 1973).

NAC art is a thriving form of commitment and celebration in the Native American Church. Pictured here is a painting entitled Morning Peyote, 1969, by Comanche Rance Hood. Photo courtesy of Rance Hood.

References

Aberle, D.F. (1966). *The Peyote Religion among the Navaho.* Chicago: Aldine Publishing Company.

Albaugh, B. and Anderson, P. (1974). Peyote in the treatment of alcoholism among American Indians. *American Journal of Psychiatry, 131*:1247-1250.

Bergman, R.I. (1971). Navaho peyote use: Its apparent safety. *American Journal of Psychiatry, 128*(6):695-9.

Blum, K., Futterman, S.L. and Pascarosa, P. (1977). Peyote, a potential ethno-pharmacological agent for alcoholism and other drug dependencies: Possible biochemical rationale. *Clinical Toxicology, 11*(4):459-72.

Brecher, E. (1972). *Licit and Illicit Drugs.* Boston: Little, Brown and Company.

Garrity, J. (2000). Jesus, peyote, and the holy people: Alcohol abuse and the ethos of power in Navajo Healing. *Medical Anthropology Quarterly, 14*(4):521-542.

Hagan, W.T. (1993). *Quanah Parker, Comanche Chief.* Norman, OK: University of Oklahoma Press.

Hertberg, H. (1971). *The Search for an American Indian Identity: Modern Pan-Indian Movements.* Syracuse, N.Y.: Syracuse University Press.

Hill, T.W. (1990). Peyotism and the control of heavy drinking: The Nebraska Winnebego in the early 1900's. *Human Organization, 49*(3):255-265.

Jackson, C. And Jackson, G. (1963). *Quanah Parker, Last Chief of the Comanches.* New York: Exposition Press.

LaBarre, W. (1947). Primitive Psychotherapy in Native American Cultures: Peyotism and Confession. *Journal of Abnormal and Social Psychology, XLII:294-309.*

LaBarre, W. (1974). *The Peyote Cult* (fourth edition). NY: Schocken Books.

McLoughlin, W.G. (1990). Ghost dance movements: Some thoughts on definition based on Cherokee history. *Ethnohistory, 37*(Winter):25-44.

Pascarosa, P and Futterman, S. (1976). Ethnopsychedlic therapy for alcoholics: Observations on the peyote ritual of the American Indian Church. *Journal of Psychedelic Drugs, 8*:215.

Pascarosa, P., Futterman, S. And Halsweig, M. (1976). Observations of alcoholics in the peyote ritual: A pilot study. *Annals of the New York Academy of Science, 273*:518-24.

Quintero, G. (1992). *Walking the Good Road: Alcoholism Recovery in the Native American Church.* Flagstaff, AZ: Northern Arizona University.

Radin, P. Ed. (1926, 1983). *Crashing Thunder: The Autobiography of an American Indian.* Lincoln, NE: University of Nebraska Press.

Roseman, B. (1963). *The Peyote Story.* Hollywood, CA: Wilshire Book, Co.

Roy, C., Choudhuri, A. and Irvine, D. (1970). The prevalence of mental disorders among Saskatchewan Indians. *Journal of Cross-cultural Psychology, 3:*383-392.

Roy, C. (1973). Indian peyotists and alcohol. *American Journal of Psychiatry, 130:*329-330.

Rudgley, R. (1994). *Essential Substances: A Cultural History of Intoxicants.* NY: Kodansha International.

Schleiffer, H. (1973). *Sacred Narcotic Plants of the New World Indians: An Anthology of Texts from the Sixteenth Century to Date.* NY: Hafner Press.

Schultes, R. (1972). An overview of hallucinogens in the Western Hemisphere. In Furst, P. *Flesh of the Gods: The Ritual Use of Hallucinogens.* NY: Praeger.

Slotkin, J.S. (1956). *The Peyote Religion: A Study of Indian-White Relations.* New York: Octagon Books.

Stewart, O.C. (1987). *Peyote Religion: A History.* Norman, OK: University of Oklahoma Press.

Morning Vision, 1973 by Terry Saul, Choctaw/Chickasaw is another example of NAC art. Photo courtesy of Terry Saul estate.

Chapter Eleven

The Ghost Dance Movements and the Sun Dance and Gourd Dance

Before leaving the abstinence-based religious and cultural revitalization movements founded in the eighteenth and nineteenth centuries, it is important to note other Native religious movements and ceremonies that while not specifically founded as therapeutic movements to heal the personal and collective effects of alcoholism, did go on to play a role in the history of recovery in Native America.

The Ghost Dance religion did not address the issue of alcohol as prominently as some of the earlier movements we have described, but its early leaders, particularly Wovoka, called upon Native People to abstain from alcohol and other drugs (Duran and Duran,1995). Wovoka (also known as Jack Wilson), a Paiute Indian, founded the Ghost Dance Religion following a vision he had during an eclipse of the sun on January 1, 1889. Wovoka was born about 1860. He worked on the ranch of David Wilson, taking on the name of Jack Wilson with the job. He and his wife and son lived in traditional Paiute style. It was on January 1, 1889, in the midst of an eclipse of the sun, that Wavoka felt his soul fly to heaven. He reported hearing the words of the Great Spirit calling him to preach (Kehoe, 1989). Wovoka called for Indians to reject the white man's ways, particularly alcohol. His new religion focused on meditation, prayer, chanting, and dancing (Waldman, 1988). It offered daily prescriptions for living a "clean, honest life," as well as hope for the future of Indian People. Wovoka prophesied a coming time when all Native People, living and dead, would be reunited without the scourges that white people had brought to their lands. He called for preparation for this time by living a code of morality and by performing new ceremonial rituals, the centerpiece of which was a circle dance that produced via exhaustion and visions, visitations and messages from the dead (Moses, 1979).

Wovoka (Jack Wilson), Paiute, in the late 1880's at the time the Ghost Dance was beginning to sweep the Plains Tribes.
Photo courtesy Smithsonian National Archives

Ghost dance religious movements were particularly prominent among the Plains Indians between 1865-1890. Wovoka's new religion entered Native history on the heels of a new Federal Indian policy issues by President William Henry Harrison that no longer recognized the political legitimacy of the tribes, called for the absorption of Indians into the nation, and called upon Indians to abandon their cultures and embrace the American lifestyle, "peaceably if they will, forcibly if they must" (Kehoe, 1989, p. 14). The Dawes Act, enacted in 1887, increased the pressure on Indian People to embrace the American way of life by making it possible for an individual Native American to own tribal land in his own name, separate from the tribe, thereby weakening the communal ownership that is more in keeping with tribal culture. The Dawes Act went a long way to breaking up the reservations when Indian land passed into non-Indian ownership by this pathway. It was not repealed until 1934 (Utter, 1993).

A painting of the Ghost Dance on the Northern Plains in the late 1880's done from a composite of photographs taken by ethnologist James Mooney. Painting by Mary Wright. Photo courtesy Smithsonian Institution

The Sun Dance ceremony was being performed by the Plains Algonquins as early as 1700, evolved into the most elaborate of the Plains Indian ceremonies of the 1800s, and was revived in the early 1900s (Jorgensen, 1972). It took place secretly throughout the early 20th century as traditional religion was effectively banned by the federal government and resumed openly again in the 1960's. The ceremony went by many tribal names, including Offerings Lodge, New Life Lodge, Abstaining from Water Dance, and Willow Dance (Hirschfelder and Molin, 2000, pp. 289-290).

A Sun Dance ground on the Northern Plains in 2003. The central Sun Dance Tree is covered with prayer cloth given as commitments by all connected with, or pledging the Sun Dance. The Sun Dance Arbor is a brush arbor constructed in a circle around the Sun Dance Tree and the dancers. It provides shade for those in the community of family, friends or tribal members either supporting a Dancer, or simply in attendance.

It was originally performed as a preparation for war or the bison hunt, but the ritual evolved following the military defeat of the Plains Indians and the loss of the bison, to focus on the personal and community renewal and the resolution of personal and community problems (Jilek, 1978a). Imbedded within an elaborate mythology, the several-day ceremony, although varying by tribe, often consisted of self-purification (sweat lodge), making vows, dancing, drumming, singing, gift-giving, abstaining from food and water, and receiving instructions from orators. In its original form, the male dancers pierced and tied their skin to a ceremonial pole around which they danced for three days and nights (Hall, 1986).

The Sun Dance is relevant to our story because of the Sun Dance proscriptions regarding alcohol. Prospective Sun dancers are instructed to abstain from alcohol because alcohol is evil and incompatible with the Sun Dance. The Sun Dance is a call to live a sober, moral life--to live the "Indian way" (Jorgensen, 1972). The preparation and ceremonial rituals of the Sun Dance extolled such values as generosity, bravery, honesty, and fortitude (Hirschfelder and Molin, 2000). A revival of the Sun Dance began in the late 1950s and spread to many Plains tribes during the 1960s. It continues to be held today among the Lakota and other tribes. It continues to serve as a reaffirmation of tribal identity and a means of acquiring personal power (Lewis, 1990).

Many forms of the Gourd Dance festival were held among Prairie and High Plains Native tribes during pre-reservation days. The early Gourd Dance ritual as practiced by the Comanche, Shoshone, Kiowa, Cheyenne, Arapaho and the Omaha included such elements as an opening invocation, speeches, drumming, bugle songs, dancing performed by various warrior societies, and gift-giving. The ceremony takes its name from the rattles used in conjunction with the dancing (Howard, 1976). It often takes place today as a notable ceremonial and spiritual dance prior to the social dancing portions of contemporary powwows.

Gourd Dancers at the Council Tree powwow in Colorado in 2004.

Accounts of contemporary recovery movements in Native America illustrate how the revival of Native spirituality and traditions is serving as an antidote to alcoholism (Suzukama, 1990). James Howard's study of the modern revival of the Gourd Dance includes accounts of how some have used the ceremony as a vehicle of personal transformation.

> *I used to be an alcoholic, and not considered of much account. I didn't go to dances much, and when I did no one paid any attention to me. Since I have taken up Gourd dancing my whole life has changed. When I go places now everyone knows me, and they treat me with great respect...I don't drink any more and I have lots of friends* (Howard, 1976, p. 255).

This sign at a Bureau of Indian Affairs boarding school demonstrates how Native Ceremony and Culture were in fact discouraged, if not outright illegal during almost the first two-thirds of the twentieth Century. Photo courtesy University of Nebraska Press.

Dr. Wolfgang Jilek (1977, 1978a,1978b, 1981), a psychiatrist, has described the potential therapeutic effects of ceremonies like the spirit dance ceremony, the Sun Dance and the Gourd Dance and the potential value in the cross-cultural collaboration between Western and Native healers in the treatment of alcoholism and other behavioral health disorders. According to Jilek (1981), rituals such as the Sun Dance and the Gourd Dance provide a number of therapeutic mechanisms:

1) providing cultural role models of sobriety (most prominent ritualists are total abstainers);

2) revering abstinence in preparation for and during the ceremonial season;

3) stigmatizing intoxication by excluding those under the influence from participation in ceremonies; and

4) incorporating activities (e.g., Indian sports) in tandem with ceremonies that are incompatible with drinking.

Collectively, Native ceremonies increase one's personal power, affirm personal/cultural identity and values, elevate self-esteem, strengthen interpersonal supports and one's bond to a larger community. They provide a way to transform a wounded community into a healing community. The healing community creates a sanctuary where personal healing occurs, just as the recovery of the individual feeds the sobriety and strength of the community.

References

Duran, E. and Duran, B. (1995). *Native American Postcolonial Psychology.* Albany, NY: State University of New York Press.

Hall, R.L. (1986). Alcohol treatment in American Indian populations: An indigenous treatment modality compared with traditional approaches. *Annals of the New York Academy of Sciences, 472*:168-178.

Hirschfelder, A. and Molin, P. (2001). *Encyclopedia of Native American Religion.* New York: Checkmark Books.

Howard, J.H. (1976). The Plains gourd dance as a revitalization movement. *American Ethnologist, 3*:243-259.

Jilek, W.G. (1977). A quest for identity: therapeutic aspects of the Salish Indian guardian spirit ceremonial. *J. Op. Psychiat, 8*(2):46-51.

Jilek, W.G. (1978a). Native renaissance: The survival of indigenous therapeutic ceremonials among North American Indians. *Transcultural Psychiatric Research, 15*:117-147

Jilek, W.G. and Jilek-Aall, L. (1978b). The psychiatrist and his shaman colleague: cross-cultural collaboration with traditional Amerindian therapists. *J. Op. Psychiat, 9*(2):32-39.

Jilek-Aall, L. (1981). Anomic depression, alcoholism and a culture-congenial Indian response. *Journal of Studies on Alcohol,* Supplement No. 9, 159-170.

Jorgensen, J. (1972). *The Sun Dance Religion.* Chicago: University of Chicago.

Kehoe, A. (1989). *The Ghost Dance: Ethnohistory and Revitalization.* New York: Holt, Rinehart and Winston.

Lewis, Thomas (1990). *The Medicine Men: Oglala Sioux Ceremony and Healing.* Lincoln, NE: University of Nebraska

Moses, L.G. (1979). Jack Wilson and the Indian Service: The response of the BIA to the Ghost Dance Prophet. *American Indian Quarterly, 5*(4):295-316.

Suzukamo, L. (1990). Spirituality helps Indians "stay on the red road". *Saint Paul Pioneer Press,* April 29, p. 1,8.

Utter, J. (1993). *American Indians—Answers to Today's Questions.* Lake Ann, MI: National Woodlands

Waldman, Carl (1988). *Encyclopedia of Native American Tribes.* New York: Facts on File Publications.

Part Three: The Red Road to Wellbriety–
A Continuing History of Resistance and Recovery

We now have circles of wellness activities that have sprung up in many of the communities. Those centers in the communities are expanding. As this develops, we always try to listen to the grassroots so we may create what needs to be placed into their hands.

—Don Coyhis

A Native American Wellbriety Talking Circle in Albuquerque, NM in 2000.

Chapter Twelve

The "Indianization" of Alcoholics Anonymous: Culturally-Congenial Alcoholism Treatment and the Rise of Community Recovery Movements

There are three historical bridges between the abstinence-based religious and cultural revitalization movements of the eighteenth, nineteenth and early twentieth centuries and the emergence and maturation of a vibrant Wellbriety movement in Indian Country. These historical links are the growth and adaptation of Alcoholics Anonymous within Native tribes, the emergence of culturally-oriented treatment for Native alcohol problems, and community recovery movements popularized by the experience of the Alkali Lake Band of the Shuswap Indians of British Columbia, Canada.

The "Indianization of Alcoholics Anonymous"– The Red Road and Talking Circles

When Alcoholics Anonymous (A.A.) first reached Indian communities, there were questions about A.A.'s appropriateness and effectiveness among Native Americans. Early suggestions that A.A. was not appropriate for American Indians and Alaska Natives have been challenged by a series of subsequent events:

- The emergence of A.A. Literature for Native Americans (*A.A. for the Native North American*, 1989)
- Native adaptations of A.A.'s Twelve Steps (Coyhis, 1990, 1999, 2000)
- Native adaptations of A.A. meeting rituals (Jilek-Aall, 1981)
- the growth of A.A. meetings conducted in Native languages,
- an annual National/International Native American Indian A.A. (NAIAA) convention (beginning in 1990), and
- the founding of the Native American Indian General Service Board of Alcoholics Anonymous (NAIGSO-AA), 1999.

The introduction of A.A. in Native American communities followed the Bureau of Indian Affairs' Relocation Program of 1953. Indians exposed to A.A. in urban treatment centers during the early 1950s introduced A.A. to other urban Native Americans and brought A.A. back to rural reservations (Womack, 1996). In the half-century since this process began, three overlapping stages are evident. In the first, Native Americans participated in "standard" A.A. meetings. Several factors enhanced this early participation in A.A. There were no fees or restrictive admission criteria and A.A.'s emphasis on spirituality was very congruent with Native cultures. However, there were concerns that some aspects of the A.A. program prevented broader Native involvement in A.A.. These concerns included A.A.'s Christian overtones, its expectation for public disclosure of personal problems, and A.A.'s predominantly Caucasian demography.

Native American Indian General Service Office of Alcoholics Anonymous (NAIGSO-AA)

"Lifting the Silence" - permission to use artwork from Sam E.

The Native American Indian General Service Office of Alcoholics Anonymous functions to provide a vision of recovery, unity and service to the more than 500 sovereign Indian Nations in North America, which are recognized by the Federal Government. Please browse the links for information about our purpose, services, events and how to register with us.

NAIGSO-AA
P.O. Box 1253
Lakeside, CA 92040
[phone] 909-927-2626
www.naigso-aa.org

Information from the website of the NAIGSO-AA (Native American Indian General Service Organization—Alcoholics Anonymous) demonstrating the accessibility and availability of Indian AA since its revitalization in the late 1980's. Courtesy of NAIGSO-AA

Two overlapping stages followed: the adaptation of A.A. for Native Americans and the development of broader cultural frameworks of recovery within Indian communities. A.A.'s influence in Native American communities increased significantly when Indians began hosting and adapting their own A.A. meetings (Jilek-Aall, 1984). The first exclusively Native American A.A. group was started in Oneida, Wisconsin in 1953. By 1966, there were 20 Indian A.A. groups in the United States. The subsequent "Indianization of A.A." was marked by the revision of A.A.'s Twelve Steps to incorporate Native ideas and language and an alternation of the structure and rituals of A.A. meetings. So-called "Indian A.A." meetings have developed their own character within local tribes. Seen as a whole, they often start late and end late; provide long breaks for socializing; include family members and children; impose no time limits for speakers; integrate A.A. and Native cultural ideas and slogans; replace references to the Christian "God" with "the Creator" or "Great Spirit"; and replace the affirmation of "powerlessness" with a focus on the acquisition of power over personal and tribal life (Jilek-A.A.ll, 1981; Womak, 1996; Simonelli, 1993). A Seneca man describes one such adaptation in his local community.

> *We call our gatherings in London (Ontario, Canada) the Medicine Wheel Healing Circle 12 Step Journey, or the Medicine Wheel Healing Circle Alcohol Awareness Meeting. We begin with a smudge, which is like the A.A. moment of silence. It's up to the Chair if he or she wants to do the Serenity Prayer. Then we go into the readings, but we use the Medicine Wheel and the 12 Steps instead of the A.A. Big Book. We then read from the A.A. 12 Traditions and do a reading from the Meditations with Native American Elders book. We take the Eagle feather and it goes all the way around the Circle so every one's had a turn to talk. Our Circles have about 25 people and take about an hour-and-a-half, with one break. We usually have 3 or 4 topics going. We have now been doing these Circles for about 7*

years...Our work in the Medicine Wheel Healing Circle 12 Step Journey is continuing (Dan S., 2004 Interview).

Approximately two percent of the current U.S. membership of Alcoholics Anonymous is Native American—23,200 out of a total membership of 1.16 million U.S. members (Alcoholics Anonymous, 2002).

Logo for an NAIGSO-AA convention held in Michigan in July of 2005. The center of the design shows North America riding on top of a turtle's back. Turtle Island is the indigenous name for North America. Courtesy of NAIGSO-AA

A significant milestone in the "Indianization" of A.A. was the publication of a Native adaptation of the basic text of Alcoholics Anonymous. Published by White Bison, Inc. in 2002, *The Red Road to Wellbriety* contains Native frameworks and stories of alcoholism recovery. The publication of this book reflects a growing tradition of Indian Peoples claiming and sharing their own stories of addiction and recovery (Maracle, 1993; Kifaru Productions, 1996).

In some locations, the healing rituals of A.A. have been incorporated into larger frameworks of addiction recovery and spiritual health. Examples of these larger frameworks include the development of the "Red Road" philosophy of Gene Thin Elk and "talking circles" that provide a healing framework for a broad spectrum of problems (Ben, 1991). The Red Road calls for detoxification of the spirit as well as the body and extols culture as a potential vehicle of personal transformation (Thin Elk, 1981).

Gene Thin Elk stands before an artwork depicting a mounted warrior riding the Red Road.
Photo credit Mark Maxon

Culturally-guided Treatment of Native American Alcohol Problems

As the history of pre-A.A. recovery circles in Native America and the growth of "Indianized" A.A. meetings became more widely known in Native communities and professional alcoholism treatment circles, questions began to be raised about what these culturally nuanced frameworks of recovery offered to Native Americans that traditional alcoholism treatment had not. It was concluded that these culturally-rooted recovery frameworks offered a striking list of therapeutic functions:

- *Commitment*: a cultural rationale for radical abstinence.
- *Purification*:   rituals of physical and emotional detoxification.
- *Identity*: affirmation of personal and cultural identity (pride of ancestral traditions, of contemporary culture, and in being Indian).

- *Reconciliation*: mending of family and social relationships.
- *Belief*: a reconstruction of values and daily lifestyle (e.g., Peyote Way, the Red Road).
- *Re-connection*: sustained affiliation with a network of recovering people and a larger cultural community.
- *Ceremony*: participation in rituals that solidify pro-recovery values and relationships.
- *Stories*: the transmission of life-changing ideas through the sharing of ancestral and contemporary stories (Coyhis & White, 2002).

Recognition of the power of culture and community in the recovery process prompted traditional alcoholism treatment programs to adapt their programs for greater cultural relevance to Native Americans, and prompted the growth of Native-sponsored treatment programs.

Native alcoholism treatment programs evolved administratively through the Office of Economic Opportunity in the 1960s, the National Institute on Alcohol Abuse and Alcoholism in the early 1970s, the Indian Health Service's Office of Alcoholism Programs (beginning in 1976), Federal Title IV legislation in 1986 (Public Law 99-570, 1986), and, more recently, toward tribal sponsorship. Through these transitions, treatment programs that serve Native populations have begun to incorporate more culturally-informed philosophies and techniques (Mills, 2003). These programs are linking treatment to Native communities via tribal sponsorship, involving tribal elders as advisors and teachers, integrating Native healers into the treatment team, recruiting and training Native addiction counselors, incorporating teachings of the Elders and the Clan Mothers within the treatment process, and using history and culture as tools of liberation (Coyhis & White, 2003; White 2004). They are also incorporating culturally-grounded ideas such as Medicine Wheel teachings; traditional ceremonies like the Sacred Pipe and spirit dances; purification and healing rituals such as the sweat lodge and the peyote ritual; and engaging kinship and community networks for long-term recovery support (Anderson, 1992; Abbott, 1998; McCormick, 2000).   Culturally-informed treatment of Native alcohol problems is grounded in tribal values and ways.   Compared to traditional treatment, it utilizes less confrontation and questioning, is quieter (less pressure for self-disclosure and more respectful of silence), and places greater emphasis on spirituality (French, 2000).

Culturally-informed treatment seeks to understand the wounded individual in the context of the historical and continued wounding of the Native tribal culture of which he or she is a part.   It recognizes that, as *The Red Road to Wellbriety* teaches, "healthy seeds cannot grow in diseased soil." (White Bison, Inc., 2002) It seeks not just the healing of the individual, but the healing of the community within which that individual is nested. As such, the goal of culture-congenial alcoholism treatment is viewed as a restoration of harmony between the individual, the family, the tribe, and the world. In contrast to interventions grounded in Western medicine, it is more holistic—more focused on creating a better person in the context of family and clan than on symptom suppression. Ernie Benedict, a Mohawk elder, explains:

> *The difference that exists is that the White doctor's medicines tend to be very mechanical. The person is repaired but he is not better than he was before. It is possible in the Indian way to be a better person after going through a sickness followed by the proper medicine* (Quoted in Jilek, 1978).

Efforts are emerging to elicit solutions to alcohol problems—at both personal and cultural levels—from the very heart of Native communities. These efforts are creating treatment hybrids that blend Native and Eurocentric methods of treating alcohol problems as well as approaches that utilize purely Native frameworks for the resolution of such problems (see Jilek, 1978, 1994; Jilek-Aall, 1981; Weibel-Orlando, 1987; Womak, 1996). While this expanded variety of treatment approaches has generated considerable support, there are calls to more rigorously evaluate both mainstream and culturally indigenous methods of treating Native alcohol problems (Weibel-Orlando, 1989; Mail & Heurtin-Roberts, 2002). Evaluations to date of Native alcoholism programs suggest that those programs with the greatest promise have four characteristics:

1) they emerge from and are operated by local tribes,

2) they are led by charismatic Native Americans whose own lives stand as a living testament to the transformative power of recovery,

3) they involve Native People seeking recovery as service recipients and peer-based service providers, and

4) they define themselves as a healing community rather than as an agency or a business (Mail & Shelton, 2002).

Community Recovery Movements

No tribal response to alcohol problems has garnered more public and professional notice than that of the community of Alkali Lake, British Columbia. The Shuswap tribal community in Alkali Lake was so plagued with alcohol problems that surrounding communities referred to it as "Alcohol Lake." The change began in 1971 when Phyllis and Andy Chelsea made a commitment to stop drinking and to confront the pervasive alcohol problems within their community. When Andy Chelsea was subsequently elected Chief of the Shuswap Tribe, he began promoting A.A. meetings, arresting bootleggers (including his own mother), confronting the drunkenness of public officials, and staging interventions to get community members into treatment. Tribal traditions were revitalized for both the adults and children of the community. Educational and job development programs were initiated for those in recovery. Over a period of ten years, this sustained effort reduced the prevalence of alcohol problems from nearly 100 percent of the tribe to less than 5 percent (Chelsea and Chelsea, 1985; Taylor, 1987). The story of the revitalization of Alakli Lake was captured in a documentary film, *The Honour of All*, directed by Canadian filmmaker Phil Lucas. The film inspired, and continues to inspire, sobriety-based cultural revitalization movements among indigenous peoples throughout the world (Ben, 1991).

The proclamation of Chief Andy Chelsea that "the community is the treatment center" (quoted in Abbot, 1998) illustrates a collectivist, as opposed to individualistic, approach to the resolution of alcohol problems. Native frameworks of recovery have always been, and continue to be, framed in terms of an inextricable link between hope for the individual and hope for a community and a people. Two and a half centuries of Native recovery movements, the current sobriety of Alkali Lake, the growing vitality of the contemporary Wellbriety Movement, and the infusion of tribal beliefs and ceremonies into alcoholism treatment programs all provide a compelling lesson: **the most effective and enduring solutions to Native alcohol problems are ones that emerge from the very heart of tribal cultures.**

The second half of the twentieth century witnessed a number of significant responses to alcohol problems in Native communities. Among the most important of these trends were the spread and "Indianization" of Alcoholics Anonymous in Native communities, the development of culturally congenial approaches to the treatment of Native alcohol problems, and the rise of abstinence-based revitalization movements within Native communities. Viewed collectively, these trends reflect new ways of understanding:

- the source of Native alcohol problems, (e.g., the intergenerational transmission of unresolved historical trauma) (Brave Heart & DeBruyn, 1998; Brave Heart, 2003; Whitbeck, et al, 2004),
- the solutions to Native alcohol problems, (e.g., cultural revitalization, cultural reconnection, participation in traditional healing practices) (Spicer, 2001), and

- the role Native values can play in the prevention and resolution of alcohol-related problems for individuals, families and communities (Flores, 1985-1986).

These understandings set the stage for the rise of a new recovery movement—a Wellbriety Movement—that has brought healing winds to Native communities across North America. In the next chapter, we will explore the history of this remarkable movement.

References

Abbott, P.J. (1998). Traditional and western healing practices for alcoholism in American Indians and Alaskan Natives. *Substance Use and Misuse,* 33(13):2605-2646.

Alcoholics Anonymous (1989). *A.A. for the Native North American.* New York: A.A. World Services.

Alcoholics Anonymous (2002). *Alcoholics Anonymous 2001 Membership Survey.* New York: A.A. World Services.

Anderson, E.N. (1992). A Healing Place: Ethnographic notes on a treatment centre. *Alcoholism Treatment Quarterly,* 9(3-4):1-21.

Ben, L.W. (1991). Wellness circles: The Alkali Lake model in community recovery processes. Doctoral dissertation, Northern Arizona University, Flagstaff.

Brave Heart, M.Y.H. & DeBruyn, L.M. (1998). The American Indian holocaust: Healing historical unresolved grief. *American Indian and Alaska Native Mental Health Research,* 8(2), 64-87.

Brave Heart, M.Y.H. (2003). The historical trauma response among Natives and its relationship with substance abuse: A Lakota illustration. *Journal of Psychoactive Drugs,* 35(1), 7-13.

Chelsea, P & Chelsea, A. (1985). *Honour of All: The People of Alkali Lake.* (Video) British Columbia, Canada: The Alkali Lake Tribal Council.

Coyhis, D. (1990). *Recovery from the Heart: A Journey through the Twelve Steps: A Workbook for Native Americans.* Center City, Minnesota: Hazelden.

Coyhis, D. (1999). *The Wellbriety Journey: Nine Talks by Don Coyhis.* Colorado Springs, CO: White Bison, Inc.

Coyhis, D. (2000). Culturally Specific Addiction Recovery for Native Americans. In: Krestan, J. Ed., *Bridges to Recovery.* New York: The Free Press, pp. 77-114.

Coyhis, D. & White, W. (2002) Addiction and recovery in Native America: Lost history, enduring lessons. *Counselor,* 3(5):16-20.

Coyhis, D. & White, W. (2003) Alcohol problems in Native America: Changing paradigms and clinical practices. *Alcoholism Treatment Quarterly,* 3/4:157-165.

Dan S., (2004). Internal correspondence, White Bison, Inc., Colorado Springs, CO.

Flores, P.J. (1985-1986). Alcoholism treatment and the relationship of Native American cultural values to recovery. *The International Journal of the Addictions*, 201 (11 & 12), 1707-1726.

French, L.A. (2000). *Addictions and Native Americans.* Westport, CT: Praeger.

Hall, R.L. (1986). Alcohol treatment in American Indian populations: An indigenous treatment modality compared with traditional approaches. *Annals of the New York Academy of Sciences,* 472:168-178.

Jilek, W.G. (1978). Native renaissance: The survival of indigenous therapeutic ceremonials among North American Indians. *Transcultural Psychiatric Research,* 15:117-147.

Jilek-Aall, L. (1981). Acculturation, alcoholism, and Indian-style Alcoholics Anonymous. *Journal of Studies of Alcohol,* (Suppl.) 9: 143-158.

Jilek, W. (1994). Traditional healing in the prevention and treatment of alcohol and drug abuse. *Transcultural Psychiatric Research* Review, 31:219-256.

Kifaru Productions (1996). *The Red Road to Sobriety—Video Talking Circle.* San Francisco, CA: Kifaru Productions.

Mail, P.D. & Heurtin-Roberts, S. (2002). Where do we go from here? Unmet research needs in American Indian alcohol use. In: In P. D. Mail, S. Heurtin-Roberts, S. Martin, & J. Howard (Eds.), *Alcohol Use Among American Indians and Alaska Natives* (NIA.A.A Research Monograph No. 37) (pp.459-486). Bethesda, MD: National Institute on Alcohol Abuse and Alcoholism.

Mail, P.D. & Shelton, C. (2002). Treating Indian alcoholics. In: In P. D. Mail, S. Heurtin-Roberts, S. Martin, & J. Howard (Eds.), *Alcohol Use Among American Indians and Alaska Natives* (NIA.A.A Research Monograph No. 37) (pp.141-184). Bethesda, MD: National Institute on Alcohol Abuse and Alcoholism.

Maracle, B. (1993). *Crazywater: Native Voices on Addiction and Recovery.* Toronto, Ontario: Viking.

McCormick, R. (2000). Aboriginal traditions in the treatment of substance abuse. *Canadian Journal of Counseling,* 34(1):25-32.

Milles, P.A. (2003). Incorporating Yup'ik and Cup'ik Eskimo traditions into behavioral health treatment. *Journal of Psychoactive Drugs,* 35(1), 85-88.

Public Law 99-570. 1986 *Indian Alcohol and Substance Abuse Prevention and Treatment Act of 1986* Section 4201, [25 U.S.C. 2401-2478]

Simonelli, R. (1993). White Bison presents a Native view: Alcoholic recovery and the Twelve Steps. *Winds of Change,* 8(3):41-46.

Spicer, P. (2001). Culture and the restoration of self among former American Indian drinkers. *Social Science & Medicine,* 53, 227-240.

Taylor, V. (1987). The triumph of the Alkali Lake Indian band. *Alcohol Health and Research World,* Fall, 57.

Thin Elk, G. (1993). Walking in balance on the Red Road. *Journal of Emotional and Behavior Problems,* 2(3), 54-57.

Weibel-Orlando, J. (1987). Culture-specific treatment modalities: Assessing client-to-treatment fit in Indian alcoholism programs. In W. Cox (Ed.), *Treatment and Prevention of Alcohol Problems: A Resource Manual.* Orlando, FL: Academic Press.

Weibel-Orlando, J. (1989). Hooked on healing: Anthropologists, alcohol and intervention. *Human Organization, 48*(2), 148-155.

Whitbeck, L.B., Chien, X., Hoytm D.R. & Adams, G.W. (2004). Discrimination, historical loss and enculturation: Culturally specific risk and resiliency factors for alcohol abuse among American Indians. *Journal of Studies on Alcohol,* July, pp. 409-418.

White, W. (2004) Native American addiction: A response to French. *Alcoholism Treatment Quarterly,* 22(1), 93-97.

White Bison, Inc. (2002). The Red Road to Wellbriety: In the Native American Way, Colorado Springs, CO: White Bison, Inc.

Womak, M.L. (1996). The Indianization of Alcoholics Anonymous: An examination of Native American recovery movements. Master's thesis, Department of American Indian Studies, University of Arizona.

Chapter Thirteen

The Modern Wellbriety Movement:
Birth of the Wellbriety Movement

Native Americans resisted the effects of alcohol on themselves and their communities throughout the first half of the twentieth century in a number of different ways. Some participated in the Native American Church, an intertribal spirituality that has over 250,000 adherents today. Others secretly kept alive their own tribe's traditional culture and spirituality even though it was effectively declared illegal by the US government for over half a century. Still others found the strength and inner resources to resist alcohol through family, community, Christianity, or other means available to them. But it wasn't until after World War II that numbers of Native American people began to find their way to the still relatively new Alcoholics Anonymous, receiving yet another means to resist alcohol and find recovery.

The Native sobriety movement has its roots in the early 1950's with Indian participation in AA. It picks up momentum through the 1960's and 1970's with the help of Indian civil rights legislation. New federal laws began to make it possible once again for Native

Americans to practice their tribal cultures and religions without interference. The availability of AA, plus the renewed freedoms guaranteed by the Indian Civil Rights Act of 1968 (ICRA, 1968), as well as the American Indian Religious Freedom Act (AIRFA) of 1978 (AIRFA, 1978), finally began to tip the balance towards Indian sobriety. It is AIRFA 1978 and its Peyote, or Native American Church Amendment in 1994 that makes greater sobriety, or *Wellbriety* possible because Wellbriety is based on re-embracing cultural values, activities and ways. Before AIRFA 1978 the many elements of Native culture were, in fact, forbidden by federal policy. As the 1980's opened, the centuries-old resistance to alcohol was finally paying off in the American Indian and Alaska Native sobriety movement (Simonelli, 2004).

The Four Laws of Change

In the early 1980's, a Native American man of the Mohican Nation was at the beginning of his own hard-won sobriety. Born and raised on the Stockbridge-Munsee reservation of Wisconsin, Don Coyhis discovered through a miracle of the Great Spirit a new life within a fellowship of other people in recovery.

Looking out on his own Native North America from the vantage point of a few years of sobriety, Coyhis saw that his people were still suffering greatly from alcohol, poverty, suicide, and so many other attributes of wounded communities. What could be done to help his people? Gratitude for his sobriety and the desire to give back to those still suffering became a driving force. What could be done? What could *he* do? This Native American man understood that his people were a tribal, community-based people. What worked for the surrounding mainstream society might not necessarily work in exactly the same way for Indian communities. He realized that his people had to find positive change *as communities and as tribal Nations,* not only as individuals, if Native cultures were to break free of what was called Indian alcoholism. The next step in his desire to give back was again left to the Great Spirit.

In 1984, Don Coyhis found himself in New Mexico visiting with a Native Elder whom others said could help. It was a good visit consisting of talk, walks in the hot New Mexico sun, and lots of baloney sandwiches, Indian tacos and gourmet sardine snacks. He talked to the Elder about his own sobriety, his identity as an Indian man, and what might get beyond individual help to that which would help Indian culture as a whole. They sat under a shade arbor while the old man drew diagrams and drawings in the sand, responding to Coyhis's questions. How familiar! It was a little like an AA chalk talk, only this was *sand talk.* And something else was familiar. This old man–well, he reminded Don of the late Joe Coyhis, his own grandfather who had raised him and was such a positive influence growing up. Tears came into Don's eyes at that moment and the Elder stopped talking for a bit. They looked at one another fondly. It was then Don realized even more his identity as a Native man and the absolutely essential role that Elders played for his people.

Joe Coyhis, Mohican Nation, grandfather of Don Coyhis.

The visit was drawing to a close when Don asked the question that wouldn't form itself until then. "I know how I got sober and how to begin to heal myself," he said, "but what about our communities, our tribes, and our Indian Nations? What can we do for our people?

"Ahhh!" said the old man, wiping clean a section of the sand with a flat board. He took the branch of pinon pine he'd been using and began to draw. "There are four elements that must take place in our Indian communities if we are to heal as a people. There are four things you must know," he said.

What happened between Don Coyhis and the Elder at that point is not exactly reproducible; but later on, driving from New Mexico back to his home in Colorado Springs, Don recalled the *Four Laws of Change* the Elder gave him that day.

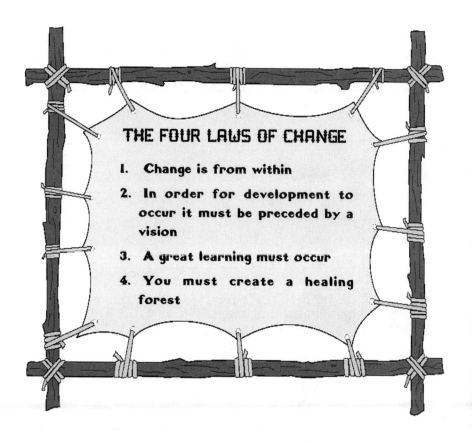

THE FOUR LAWS OF CHANGE

1. Change is from within

2. In order for development to occur it must be preceded by a vision

3. A great learning must occur

4. You must create a healing forest

The First Law, <u>Change is from within</u>, means that all meaningful and positive change starts from the inside and works its way out. Healthy change is not necessarily from the top down, or from the outside-in. Meaningful change comes right from inside us. It's about people changing themselves, with the help of the Great Spirit. The kind of change we need is from "within-side," not primarily from outside. Changing in the spiritual world manifests itself in the physical world.

The Second Law, <u>In order for development to occur it must be preceded by a vision</u>, also means that if there is no vision, then there won't be positive development. Because we were created with free will, the human being has to work with thought. The principle is, *we move towards and become like that which we think about.* If that is true, then it's important to be thinking about what we are thinking about. As we start to consciously create a vision, then things start to happen. If the community thinks about something together, that's what the community moves towards.

The Third Law, <u>A great learning must occur,</u> means that all parts of the cycle of life—baby, youth, adult and elder—within a community must participate in simultaneous learning experiences in order for the community to get well. For example, in order for the youth to get well, the community must simultaneously work on its own wellness. The Great Learning includes personal healing and self-knowledge as well as technical learning. It means that community members will participate in ongoing educational opportunities that may include conventional academic education. In Native American communities, the Great Learning includes re-learning the Native culture that may have been forgotten through years of historical trauma.

The Fourth Law, <u>You Must Create a Healing Forest,</u> is the basis of the Healing Forest Model used in many Native American community wellness and self-determination activities today

(Simonelli, 1993). The story is told of a group of sick trees in a sick forest that want to get well. The sick trees leave the forest to find treatment for their illness and do come back to health. But when they return to their forest, which symbolizes the community, they get sick once again because they are re-infected by the overwhelming conditions of the forest (community). The Fourth Law means that in order for the community to return to vitality and health, the entire community must become part of the self-development and self-determination process.

Precursors to the Wellbriety Movement

During the next few years, Don Coyhis thought about the Four Laws of Change that the Elder had given him. He also thought about other parts of their conversation having to do with the Elder's words about the Medicine Wheel. Don would learn much more about the Medicine Wheel teachings from other Elders in the years to come; but at this point he realized that his own people, from time immemorial, had lived through an understanding of interconnectedness, relatedness, and wholeness which kept their cultures well. He realized that *interconnectedness* is the basis of Medicine Wheel teachings and sought to learn more. In 1985, a blockbuster video of Indian sobriety, *The Honour of All* (Chelsea, 1985) burst on the scene to reinforce what was starting to happen in indigenous sobriety in North America. *The Honour of All* documented the beginnings of sobriety among Native people of the Alkali Lake Indian Band of Williams Lake, British Columbia. The video supported any Native person seeking sobriety. In 1988, Don Coyhis and his sobriety buddy Wayne Records founded White Bison, Inc., an American Indian non profit organization that Don would use to give back to his own people towards the ending of Indian alcoholism.

In accordance with the Four Laws of Change, White Bison was founded with the vision of achieving 95% sobriety among Indian youth by the year 2000. One of the first Native organizations to see the value and need for White Bison's vision was AISES, the

American Indian Science and Engineering Society. AISES was committed to seeing Native youth find success in the science, engineering and mathematics professions. Norbert Hill, Jr., Oneida, then Executive Director of AISES, immediately realized that the AISES youth were at risk for alcohol abuse just as other Native people. He invited Don Coyhis and White Bison to teach at each of the AISES National conferences in the 1990's. It was an AISES-sponsored event, a Gathering of Native American Elders in Loveland, Colorado in 1991 that was the Great Spirit's gift to the birth of the Wellbriety Movement.

Wellbriety means to be both sober and well. It is a word that was inspired by a Passamaquoddy Elder in Maine in 1995. For Native People, Wellbriety means to live through the principles, laws and values that indigenous cultures lived by before the European came to North America.

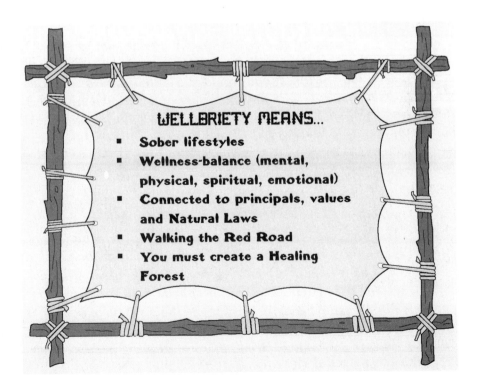

WELLBRIETY MEANS...
- **Sober lifestyles**
- **Wellness-balance (mental, physical, spiritual, emotional)**
- **Connected to principals, values and Natural Laws**
- **Walking the Red Road**
- **You must create a Healing Forest**

The Elder's Conference

In 1991, AISES sponsored an Elder's conference in Loveland, Colorado that provided Don with more of the Elders' teachings that his heart was looking for. Here is how Don Coyhis remembers the pivotal Elders Conference in 1991 (Coyhis, 2000).

"In July of 1991 we had the opportunity to bring together a group of Native American Elders from many of the different tribes. They gathered from the Oneida Nation, the Hopi Nation, the Navajo or Dine', the Nez Perce, the Blood Reserve in Canada, the Dakota Nation and from many others. We brought together this group of Elders and requested that they teach us for four days because many of those at the gathering worked in Native communities or organizations. We were discovering that the Elders have a great contribution to make to us, to our tribes, to our organizations, and to individuals.

"We asked the Elders at this conference to give us their point of view on many different subjects. We asked them, 'What is it that you would like to tell the world about what is going on with the mother earth and her inhabitants? What is it that you could tell us about building families? What is it you could tell us about communities? What is it you could tell us about relationships?'

"The Elders told us that we, as earth people, or as earth tribes, had entered into a new springtime, a new springtime of life. They told us that there was a prophecy which said we, as earth people, we as earth tribes, were destined to spend a long time in a cold winter time. This would be a time of turmoil, a time of strife, a very difficult time for the people. And the prophecy went on to say that when the sun became blocked in the seventh moon of a particular year it would be a very significant indication that the wintertime was over and that we, as earth people, would enter into a new springtime.

"In July of 1991 there was an eclipse of the sun. The Elders told us it was a very significant event. And they told us that for the next twelve moons, from that July to the next July, a great stirring was going to take place in the universe.

"They told us that through this stirring the Great Spirit was going to cause a distribution of new types of gifts, new healing gifts that would be given to many, many people. We were told that as a result of the new springtime, all of the people would begin to come together from all of the directions—from the red/brown direction, from the yellow direction, from the black direction, and from the white direction. They called this new period we were entering a 'coming together time.'

"As we discussed these things with the Elders at that gathering, we asked them about a particular community we were working in. This community was a Native American community, and in this community the average life span was 37.6 years. This particular community had just one high school graduate. It had about 85 percent serious alcoholism among people over the age of twelve, and less than eight percent of their people lived to be over 43.

"In a sense, we were asking the Elders, 'Is it too late?' Is it possible to take a community and turn it around? They told us that contrary to how things look in society and in the world—we might see a lot of confusion, a lot of abuse, a lot of dysfunction, a lot of broken families—if you have a community that is in a downward spiral, it can be brought back. That community can be brought back to what the Elders call the Red Road or the right road—the right way of thinking. They said we would be able to do that if we were to follow certain laws.

"The Elders told us that there are two states we can be in as human beings. One state of mind we can be in is the state of 'I don't know what I don't know.' If you just think about that a while, that we don't know what we don't know,

it means we could be in trouble and not know it. But they said there's another state of mind that we can get into, and that is the state of mind that goes from 'I don't know what I don't know' to 'Now I <u>know</u> what I don't know.' Once we know what we don't know, then we can go and fix it. So they told us they would share some information with us, information that perhaps we've forgotten.

"A long time ago, the Great Spirit put a system in place and that system is still here today. If we have an understanding of that system as individuals, if we start to teach our children, teach our organizations, run our tribes and run our communities according to these principles and concepts from the old days, then that would allow us to get from 'I don't know what I don't know' to 'Now I <u>know</u> what I don't know.' As we implement these principles, laws and values that the Great Spirit gave to us, they will allow us to help individuals, communities or organizations come back on track. When the Elders say, 'Walk the Red Road' they mean the big system that the Great Spirit made.

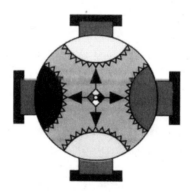

A Medicine Wheel used by White Bison, Inc. in its teachings. For more information about the Medicine Wheel see (White Bison, Inc., 2002).

"The Elders used an element called the Medicine Wheel to help us see in this new way and to walk the Red Road. The Medicine Wheel is a very ancient Native way of teaching. Not all tribes have a Medicine Wheel. Of the tribes that do have a Medicine Wheel, many of them are

different from one another. A good way to look at it is that each tribe, each nation, is like a separate country; it's a sovereign nation. Because our Native People did not have a way to write languages, the Elders of each tribe used to teach us by symbols and by pictures. So the Medicine Wheel is the way that the Elders taught us. "

Native Americans had been finding sobriety in greater numbers since the early 1950's, but some say the Wellbriety Movement really had its roots in the American Indian Religious Freedom Act of 1978. From that time onward, it was no longer illegal for Native People to practice their culture and spirituality. Wellbriety includes a return to the principles, laws and values of indigenous culture. If the Wellbriety Movement is rooted in AIRFA 1978, then its first shoots really burst from the ground with the Elder's wisdom that was presented at the Elders conference in 1991.

Prophecies, Teachings, and the Passamaquoddy Community Program

The Elders shared many Native prophecies at the meeting in 1991. They shared a prophecy going back to the early part of the 20th Century that said when the eagle circled the earth and moon it would be a sign that the long wintertime was over and a new springtime was soon to come. In 1969, the Apollo 11 Lunar Lander carried an eagle feather when it traveled to the moon. The name of the Lander itself was Eagle. Everyone knows that when the Lander touched down on the moon, astronaut Neil Armstrong said, "The eagle has landed," fulfilling the prophecy. This eagle feather was later entrusted to the AISES organization by Challenger astronaut, the late Ellison Onizuka, where it now resides in Albuquerque, New Mexico.

The Elders also said that healers would begin to emerge from all four directions or major races—the red/brown, the yellow, the black and the white—when the new springtime arrived. Their prophecies said that each race or direction had a special healing gift to share for the healing time to come, and this sharing would begin in earnest with the coming of the new springtime. The birth of multicultural diversity in the 1960's was the first time that this kind of sharing became possible, fulfilling the prophecy.

The Elders said that you would begin to see young people with old spirits emerge when the long wintertime was over. These are youth who would sound just like Elders when they spoke. They said the youth would begin to sing the old songs and would start to bring back the many indigenous languages that had been forgotten. They said you would begin to see young people sitting at the drums—young women and young men alike—and that is what is happening now. They said that when the new springtime was at hand women would once again step forward and begin to lead. They told us that their prophecies revealed a spider would build a web around the entire earth so that the interconnectedness of the Medicine Wheel teachings would be revealed through communication. That prophecy has come to pass with the arrival of the Internet. They also told us that we would know that the new springtime was at hand when a white buffalo was born.

Miracle, the white buffalo born on August 20, 1994 on the ranch of Valerie and Dave Heider in Janesville, Wisconsin.
Photo courtesy of Heider Ranch.

A white buffalo calf named Miracle was born in Janesville, Wisconsin in 1994, fulfilling the prophecy. Miracle was the first white buffalo to be born since 1933 and was visited by many, many people on the Valerie and Dave Heider Ranch in Wisconsin until her unexpected death in 2004. The coming of Miracle was both a symbol and the actual fulfillment of prophecy for the healing of First Nations people. In her short life, Miracle went through all four color phases—white, red, yellow and black—in keeping with the prophecies of the new springtime (White Bison, Inc., 2002). The excitement of her birth and the birth of the Wellbriety Movement happen almost in the same breath.

Starting in 1993, the White Bison organization began to make the teachings of the Medicine Wheel and the Elders' wisdom available to everyone. Audiocassettes were made for the Medicine Wheel teachings, and a book called "Meditations With Native American Elders" was offered (Coyhis, 1995). This was in keeping with the Third Law of Change: A Great Learning Must Occur. It is also at this time that White Bison began to merge the Medicine Wheel teachings with the 12 Steps of Alcoholics Anonymous.

Many Native Americans got sober and recovered from the effects of alcohol by attending AA from the early 1950's onward. Sometimes Indian AA groups formed in communities with a Native American population as the years went on. The Indianization of AA took place in those meetings simply because there were Indians at the meetings and Native culture was expressed through the participants. But it was in the early 1990's that Don Coyhis began to directly connect the teachings of the Medicine Wheel with the 12 Steps of Alcoholics Anonymous in his own recovery. Many Elders who learned of the 12 Steps began to say, "Yes, these 12 Steps are very similar to our own teachings." It wasn't long after he began to do this for himself and for other Native American 12 Steppers that White Bison was invited to teach a combination of Medicine Wheel teachings along with the 12 Steps to Native American men incarcerated in a prison in Idaho. This 3-day series of teachings was captured on video tape and became the basis for the Medicine Wheel and the 12 Steps Program, which would go on to be one of the roots of the Wellbriety Movement. (White Bison, Inc., 1996)

The two-year event leading to the actual term "Wellbriety" was an invitation to White Bison by the Passamaquoddy Tribe at the village of Sipayak on Pleasant Point, near Perry, Maine to present a community change program. Don Coyhis and the White Bison staff had been thinking a lot about the Healing Forest idea of the Fourth Law of Change. In order for a community to heal, all parts of the community must be in the healing process: you must create a healing forest. It takes a community to heal a community. A group of Passamoquoddys at Pleasant Point wanted to help their community heal from the many unwell behaviors in their community. Approximately 40 people committed to work a two-year White Bison program. From 1993-1995, Don Coyhis and the White Bison staff worked with this group of 40, utilizing many of the tools, methods and techniques that would go on to be part of the Wellbriety Movement.   Included were the Community Vision Day; the teachings of the Medicine Wheel; the mind mapping process; telling the community story; the community naming process; the action plan; the staking ceremony, and so many other self-determined, self-development activities embraced by the community itself.   The Sipayak group named its change process **The Healing Wind** to honor their position on the coastline of the North Atlantic, and with the idea that from this beginning a healing wind would begin to blow from east to west across Turtle Island, the Native American home (Passamaquoddy Tribe, 1996) (Simonelli, 1995)

An Elder from the Pleasant Point community suggested the word "Wellbriety" in 1994. It came from a word in the Passamaquoddy language meaning something further than sobriety and recovery from alcohol. It meant to be sober and well in a cultural way. The word couldn't be translated exactly so it was called *Wellbriety*. The Healing Wind group produced a stunning 113-page book to document the journey they all took in their two-year healing process (Passamaquoddy Tribe, 1996). Entitled <u>The Passamaquoddy Community Vision, 1996</u>, their book remains today a classic in Native American community change done by the community itself, but with the assistance of an outside Native organization. In this book, one of the Healing Wind members states very clearly the community-guided relationship that is necessary for a community in healing to go through the process in their own cultural ways. Here is what they say:

> "Don Coyhis...was invited to be our guide. His Mohican ways, his belief in Indian people, his commitment to old ways as the best way to find our future, and his own journey to wellness let us know he was a guide we could trust and learn from. With Don as our guide, we began our journey to wellness. He was asked to be a listener and teacher. He was asked to help the community learn and remember Indian ways. He was asked to share the wisdom of the elders, the depth of his wisdom, and the strength of his conviction to Indian people and their future" (Passamaquoddy Tribe, 1996, p.1).

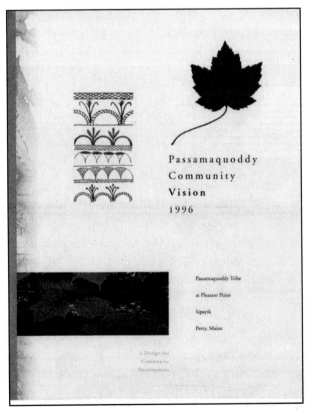

This book was created and published by the Passamaquoddy Tribe at Pleasant Point, Maine, as a direct result of the community change program led by White Bison there in the early 1990's. The book contains one of the best summaries of the Healing Forest Model and its community changes processes to date.
Photo courtesy Passamaquoddy Tribe

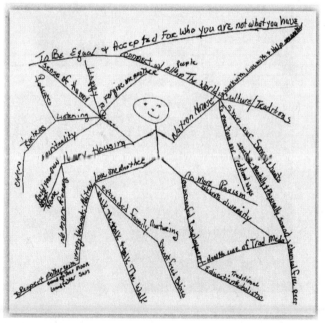

Two Mind Maps done as part of the Passamaquoddy Healing Wind community change program in the early 1990's. Mind maps would go on to be one of the tools of the various Wellbriety Movement programs in the years to come.
Photo courtesy Passamaquoddy Tribe

Telling the community story was an important part of the Passamaquody Healing Wind process. The upper photo tells a part of the community story with an old, traditional fishing wier in the background helping to create the setting. The fishing wier (lower photo) is a prominent landmark in Passamaquoddy Bay, adjacent to the village. Upper photo courtesy of the Passamaquoddy Tribe.

A photo from the Passamaquoddy book reveals a work session during the community change process at Pleasant Point. Photo courtesy Passamaquoddy Tribe

The Hoop and the First Hoop Gatherings

The Passamaquoddy community change program was still in progress in 1994 when an Indian man had a vision. "Visions often come to me about three or four in the morning," Don Coyhis recounted later. In this vision there was a circle of white light surrounded by darkness. All of a sudden something began to break out of the ground in the center of this white light and begin to grow. It was a willow sapling that began to grow, and as it grew straight and tall it then shed its leaves like in the autumn of the year. Then it bent itself into a circle, into a willow hoop. Next, he saw a small dot form itself up in the northern direction in the circle of light. The dot began to move very slowly towards the willow hoop and it soon dipped to the earth. When it came up, it had become an eagle feather that attached itself to the hoop. The same thing next happened from the eastern, southern and western directions, bringing the first four eagle feathers to the hoop. All of a sudden, other dots began appearing from all the directions until 100 eagle feathers were attached to the hoop.

When the man woke up he knew he must visit the Elders in order to understand the meaning and intent of his vision. He traveled to South Dakota where seventeen Elders talked with him for many hours in order to understand his spirit and intent, in order to look into his heart. The Elders smudged him with sage and sweetgrass, revealing that they themselves had been having visions. They said they knew someone was coming. And they said, "Build that Hoop. You are to build that Hoop of 100 eagle feathers just like in that dream, that vision."

Where would he find the 100 eagle feathers as required by the vision? Over the next year, they began to come. They arrived mysteriously by mail from Indians who had perhaps heard of the vision by way of the moccasin telegraph. They were offered when Coyhis was doing one of the many White Bison training programs somewhere in Indian Country. Sometimes meeting someone on the street led to the donation of an eagle feather. Some even came from as far away as Australia or New Zealand. By 1995 there were enough feathers to build the Hoop. During four days of sweat lodge ceremonies, the Hoop was assembled as the 100 feathers were attached to the willow hoop, which had been wrapped with the colors of the four directions. Twenty-five feathers were attached in each of the four directions. The 100 Eagle Feather Hoop was a reality.

GIFTS OF THE SACRED HOOP:
Healing • Hope • Unity and the
Power to Forgive the Unforgivable

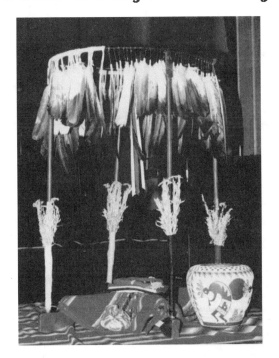

The 100 Eagle Feather Hoop of the Wellbriety Movement

The first large Hoop gathering took place in June of 1995 in Janesville, Wisconsin, the same place in which the prophesied white buffalo calf had been born during the previous month of August. This first Hoop gathering was an assembly of multicultural Elders. There were Elders present from all four directions, as well as tribal participants from these nations: Oglala Lakota; Oneida; Seneca; Passamaquoddy; Penobscot; Micmac; Ho Chunk; Nez Perce; Mohican; Menominee; Yakama; Inuit; Ojibwa; Malisette; and many more North American tribes. There were also Elders from Tibet, Africa, Australia, and Saami Elders from Norway as participants.

Many different ceremonial events marked that first gathering around the Hoop. There was a blessing ceremony, a Wiping of the Tears Ceremony, a Pipe Ceremony, a Cedar Bough Ceremony, and a Ceremony during which each person present individually placed his or her prayers for all humanity into the Hoop. As part of the ceremonies that day, the Elders placed four gifts into the Hoop. These four Gifts of the Hoop are the gifts of **Healing; Hope, Unity;** and the **Power to Forgive the Unforgivable.** These are the gifts that the Hoop carries to this day.

Community members set up the Hoop for a Hoop Journey event in Milwaukee, Wisconsin in 2003. Don Coyhis (left) assists other participants.

The next gathering to receive the gifts of the Hoop was a gathering of Native American Women in Leadership, which was held in the mountains West of Colorado Springs, Colorado in the fall of 1995. Approximately 40 women holding positions of leadership in Indian communities or organizations from around Turtle Island came to discuss their common goals of leadership and wellness for Native People; and they came to participate in a Hoop ceremony. This gathering was in accordance with the prophecy that women would begin to lead the people in the new springtime—the time whose outlines were becoming clearer and clearer now.

A poster announces the Men's Gathering in 1996. Twelve inspirational talks were given. One of the talks can be found in Appendix 2 of this book.

After the women's conference, and during that winter of 1995-96, a great new undertaking was envisioned. Indian People knew that Indian men suffered disproportionately in indigenous societies. More than the women, Native men had lost their traditional roles, which were as hunters, warriors and ceremonialists. In order to offer Native men's healing, a Gathering of Native American Men was planned for late spring of 1996. The Indian men's gathering was held in late May and early June of 1996 at a high mountain meadow called Badger flats in the mountains west of Colorado Springs, Colorado (Simonelli, 1996). About 1500 men, women and children attended and participated in the three-day event.   Tents and campsites ringed the large meadow in which the many events took place. There were Hoop ceremonies in which individuals could offer tobacco and their prayers into the Hoop, as well as many talks by male and female Elders.

Onondaga Eldei Fieida Jacques spoke at the Gathering of Native American Men in Colorado in 1996

Eight Native Elder men and two Native Elder women gave powerful inspirational presentations. Onondaga Nation member Freida Jacques referred to her Six Nations tradition of peace in a talk about the Good Mind. She said, *"The Peacemaker came and brought us principles to live by. One of those principles was the Good Mind. He changed all those people with these principles and the Good Mind. I'd like to talk about the Good Mind right now"* (Jacques, 1996). Please see Appendix 2 in this book.

Nez Perce Elder Horace Axtell gave a talk and said, *"There are so many problems all over this world. But our world that we came to, right here, is a strong world. When we stand together in a Circle we bring all our strength, our powers, our spirituality together and we become like one."* Horace Axtell's book, *A Little Bit of Wisdom* (Axtell &Aragon, 1997) published a year later went on to expand on this Wellbriety Elder's life and times. This book, and other books by First Nations Elders, offer a link to the traditional knowledge of the old ways by people who are fully living in the modern ways.

Horace Axtell, a Nez Perce Elder at the Men's Gathering in Colorado in 1996

Over 500 Native American veterans from previous wars participated in a Wiping of the Hands ceremony whose purpose was to welcome each man or woman home from war in a healing, spiritual way. This ceremony took place because the Elders said that Native Americans hadn't been welcomed back in a spiritual, ceremonial way from wars dating from World War II. They said further that this omission was one cause of the increased Indian alcoholism since 1945. Years after the men's gathering, Native men would say that this event was life changing for them because they felt welcomed back to Native society as a Native American man. One man said, *"A young boy ran away many years ago from sexual abuse, survived the rage and hurt associated with alcohol, drugs, inhalants, gangs, domestic violence, divorce, and army life overseas, and eventually found the Red Road in 1978... With continued healing and sobriety, the young boy quit running; a man came home from Colorado last summer."* All in all, 117 tribal nations were represented at the Men's Gathering. These first three great Hoop gatherings created a longing and a stirring for the Wellbriety Movement, whose shape was more rapidly becoming visible. They led directly to the four National Hoop Journeys that were still to come.

Men dance under the Hoop in an impromptu closing at the Gathering of Native American Men in 1996.

References

AIRFA (1978). American Indian Religious Freedom Act of 1978, amended to 1994: {42 U.S.C 1996, P.L. 95-341, August 11, 1978}

Axtell, H. & Aragon, M. (1997). *A Little Bit of Wisdom: Conversations With a Nez Perce Elder,* Lewiston, Idaho: Confluence Press

Chelsea, P & Chelsea, A. (1985). *Honour of All: The People of Alkali Lake.* (Video) British Columbia, Canada: The Alkali Lake Tribal Council.

Coyhis, D. (1995). *Meditations With Native American Elders.* Colorado Springs, Colorado: White Bison

Coyhis, D. (2000). Culturally specific addiction recovery for Native Americans. In: Krestan, J. Ed., *Bridges to Recovery.* New York: The Free Press, pp. 77-114

ICRA (1968). Indian Civil Rights Act of 1968. {25 U.S.C. 1968, P.L. 90-284, April 11, 1968}

Jacques, F. (1996, Autumn). The Good Mind, *Winds of Change,* 11(4), pp.154-155

Passamaquoddy Tribe (1996). *Passamaquoddy Community Vision, 1996.* Perry Maine: White Owl Press. Pleasant Point Passamaquoddy Reservation Housing Authority

Simonelli, R. (1993, Spring). The Healing Forest. *Winds of Change,* 8(2), pp18-22

Simonelli, R. (1995, Summer). The Healing Wind, *Winds of Change,* 10(3), pp16-20

Simonelli, R. (1996, Autumn). A Gathering of Native Men in Colorado, *Winds of Change,* 11(4), pp 146-150

Simonelli, R. (2004). Sobriety and American Indian history, *Well Nations Magazine,* July-August, 2004: 25-46

White Bison, Inc. (1996). *The Medicine Wheel and the 12 Steps for Men.* (Video) Colorado Springs, Colorado: White Bison, Inc.

White Bison, Inc. (2002). *The Red Road to Wellbriety: In the Native American Way.* Colorado Springs, Colorado: White Bison, Inc.

Chapter Fourteen

The Wellbriety Movement Comes of Age

The Wellbriety movement continued to grow after the Native American Men's Gathering in 1996. Both men and women left Colorado at the conclusion of the Gathering on June 3, 1996 convinced that something was really happening for Indian healing and that they were part of it. The Hoop would be taken to diverse communities, both Native and non-Native, in the next two years. Either in the care of Don Coyhis, or carried by the many volunteers of those years, the Hoop, its gifts, and the new Wellbriety teachings were eagerly awaited. It went to the Passamaquoddy Nation in September of 1996 for a ceremony celebrating the conclusion of the Healing Wind change process that began in 1993 for Pleasant Point. It went to the Tribal Health Center of the Grand Traverse Band of Odawa Indians in Michigan that October. There was a large turnout for the Hoop in Northfield, Minnesota early in 1997. The Hoop was present at many AISES Conferences from 1997 onward. The sacred Hoop ceremony became a regular part of most of the White Bison training program events in Indian communities across the nation. Wherever the Hoop went, Native Americans and other indigenous people understood the meaning of the Eagle feathers and felt the

Gifts of Healing, Hope, Unity and Forgiveness that the Hoop brought to them as individuals and to their community.

The Men's Gathering in Colorado also sparked a group on the Fort Hall Reservation in Idaho to request a Healing Forest style community change process for their community. From 1996 until 1998, the Shoshone-Bannock people experienced and participated in a community development process similar to the Passamaquoddy except that it was in keeping with their tribal history, ways and needs. There was also another difference: they had the Hoop. Most training sessions in Fort Hall included a Hoop ceremony and the presence of the Hoop during each 3-day event. During one such event in August of 1997 at Fort Hall, 11 year-old Paula Sheppard stood up confidently in a circle of youth, adults and Elders and said something that would express the desire of Native youth in Wellbriety for years to come. *"We the children like to be heard with our inside voices,"* she said. *"We want to put our own youth group together. We want to show others the way we do it. We want to spread our happiness to other people. When you spread happiness something happens; it's a good feeling."* The Fort Hall group named themselves **The Healing Rains.** Truly, a Healing Wind had begun to blow from the Northeast. It traveled southward and then westward, eventually bringing its healing gift as rain to the Fort Hall community and many communities soon to come.

Throughout 1997, the Medicine Wheel and the 12 Steps Program for men was made available by request to individuals, communities and especially for Native American Men in prison. Over one hundred 7-video tape sets of the Program were distributed to federal and state prisons across the country at the request of the institution. A 3-day training program about using the program in prison was presented in Colorado Springs in August of 1997 to about 40 addictions specialists working at both the federal and state levels. The conference was honored to have Mark Gornik, Idaho Department of Corrections, present at the conference. It was Mark's invitation early in the 1990's that enabled the Medicine Wheel and the 12 Steps program for men to be video taped at the Idaho State Prison in Pocatello. This event in 1997 ended with a Hoop

Ceremony. It was a precursor to the Wellbriety For Prisons program that would begin in 2002.

1997 was also the year that the Medicine Wheel and the 12 Steps program was taped before a group of multicultural women incarcerated at the Idaho Women's Prison in Boise. It was the same blending of the Medicine Wheel teachings of the Indian Red Road along with the 12 Steps of Alcoholics Anonymous that had been done for men, but with the advantage of over five years of honing the program (White Bison, 1998). This program also had the benefit of the Hoop. The women's program resulted in a nine-videotape set that began distribution in 1998. The women's stories are as powerful as the men's, and perhaps more heart wrenching. Who can fail to be moved by the words of one of the women there?

> *"When they slammed that door behind me and it echoed through the empty hallways here, the sadness and the separation of my heart from my family and everybody that's dear and true to me really came home then. It didn't come home when I took that first drug when I was eleven years old. It didn't come home when I was dealing those drugs and thinking that I was all cool, that I was the big bag lady. Now, it hurts every day when I wake up and I'm still here. Every day when I wake up and my children aren't there with me to hug me. It hurts. They didn't choose that. I made those choices. And they weren't good choices"* (White Bison, Inc., 1998).

1999--Circles of Recovery is Born

The Wellbriety Movement took another leap forward with the coming of Circles of Recovery in the autumn of 1998. The Circles of Recovery concept is simple. Imagine that sobriety, recovery and wellness for Indigenous people is like a pebble dropped into a lake. From the initial splash of Indians getting sober, circles would radiate out to all parts of the community, touching each part of Indian

Country with the gifts of healing. There would be a continuity of teachings, method and approach to addictions healing. Even though many good training and wellness programs had been circulating throughout Indian country since the mid-to late 1980's, it would take the Wellbriety Movement to help tie them together as a recognizable movement. Circles of Recovery came to life by way of a grant from CSAT, the Center for Substance Abuse Treatment, a part of the Substance Abuse and Mental Health Services Administration (SAMHSA) of the federal government. Not only was it a great honor for an American Indian organization to have been awarded the CSAT grant, but the honor meant something more: Wellbriety was finally affecting many American Indians and Alaska Natives, coming into the radar of the federal drug and alcohol recovery programs as an identifiable movement.

Circles of Recovery began in 1999 with key events designed to constantly pulse out the message of sobriety, recovery, healing and Wellbriety to Native Americans all across Turtle Island. With the coming of Circles of Recovery, there would be yearly Journeys of the Sacred Hoop to bring the message of Wellbriety right into Native America. A series of annual Circles of Recovery Conferences would take place so that Indians and others interested in the healing resources of the Wellbriety Movement could convene and share the good energy and best practices of the Movement. The established federal drug and alcohol recovery month celebrations that took place each September would be augmented by National Native American Wellbriety Month held concurrently each September. And the creation of a network of grassroots, community-based individuals called *Firestarters* would begin as part of Circles of Recovery. Firestarters would be people who pass the spark of healing around their communities so that the fire of wellness might light up each and every community member. Way back in 1985 the Alkali Lake documentary *The Honour of All* summed it up when it said, *"Recovery is like a fire; someone has to start it."* Grassroots Firestarters would be some of those people.

The first Hoop Journey and recruitment of Firestarters began in 1999. Hoop Journey I (1999) started with Ceremonies in the

Longhouse of the Onondaga Nation near Syracuse, New York on the cold and blustery day of March 6, 1999. It was a great honor for the Wellbriety Movement to be sent off on the first of many healing pilgrimages by the traditional Onondaga Nation. The Hoop of 100 feathers stood in the centuries-old presence of the Peacemaker, the great warrior for peace who brought the Five Nations Haudenosaunee people (Mohawk; Onondaga; Seneca; Cayuga; and Oneida) out of their own struggle long before Europeans arrived in America. The flame of wellness was handed from the Peacemaker to the Wellbriety movement at the start of an 11,000 mile, almost three-month tour. Hoop Journey I brought Wellbriety Awareness Day presentations to 27 Native American Tribal colleges and their communities scattered across the western United States and Canada.

A dancer performs at a Hoop Journey I event in Santa Fe, New Mexico in 1999

How did the coming of the Hoop affect Tribal College students and staff? Rita Alvarez, an art instructor at DQ University, then a Tribal College, spoke of the experience in California when she says, *"The Hoop was very powerful. The students and faculty ran from UC/Davis in order to connect that school with our experience. They ran almost ten miles carrying the Hoop. The gathering with the Hoop helped people to come together. The significance of the Hoop being here is that many students got very excited and curious and wanted to participate."* Hoop Journey I pulsed out the message to an estimated 7500 people, including 350 individuals who signed up to be Firestarters. During the first Hoop Journey, a condor feather from South America was placed at the center of the Hoop by Shoshone-Bannock Elder Snookins Honena, fulfilling a prophecy that said the healing time would begin when the eagle and the condor flew together.

The First Annual Circles of Recovery Conference was held in September of 1999 in Colorado Springs, Colorado. The focus of the Conference was on healing the individual. One of the landmarks of Circles of Recovery I was the presence of three Native American Elders who would support the Wellbriety Movement in the coming Hoop Journeys and conferences. Ozzie Williamson, Blackfeet Nation; Horace Axtell, Nez Perce; and Bill Iron Moccasin, Lakota, all came through their own recovery from alcohol. They offered their example, counsel and love to the thousands of people who would become involved in the Wellbriety Movement in the coming years. Ozzie Williamson summed up what a lot of people were starting to discover. *"I think Don's idea of Wellbriety or further sobriety is what has been missing,"* he said. *"When we talk about going to treatment and getting sober and staying sober it doesn't deal with the emotional aspect the way Wellbriety does. Wellbriety deals with the physical, emotional, mental and spiritual. When I first heard the word 'Wellbriety' it really caught me in a way I couldn't quite understand. Then when I learned more about what it means it made sense. You treat the whole person and the whole family."*

Circles of Recovery I introduced the Medicine Wheel and the 12 Steps Program more strongly than ever to the people. A conference participant form the Pima Nation in Arizona attested to some of the Wellbriety vision when he said, *"I got sober through AA and now I am going to bring this new cultural approach to the 12 Steps into our community. As Indian People we have to be open-minded. I work with the churches, with white people, black people, the Chinese, and Hispanics. We can all work together as one because our spirits are all connected. We have to work with everyone for our healing."* The year 1999 showcased the Wellbriety

The late Bill Iron Moccasin speaks at the first Circles of Recovery Conference in Colorado Springs, Colorado in 1999. Right is wife Carole Iron Moccasin.

Wellbriety Elders

Horace Axtell and wife Andrea in Albuquerque, New Mexico for the fourth Circles of Recovery Conference in 2003

Ozzie Williamson at the second Circles of Recovery Conference in Billings, Montana in 2002

Movement to Native America in a way that would develop and grow in years to come.

2000--A New Century

Buffalo, New York is Indian Country. The coming of a new century brought a Firestarters Program to Buffalo and its support for a Native American culture-specific recovery program at the Stutzman Addiction Treatment Center in Buffalo. Called the *Freedom Way Program,* the curriculum that Valerie Staats, Mohawk, established in the New York State center drew on all of the many Indian culture-based addictions recovery approaches that were appearing now year after year. In a typical year, about 30 of the 600 client admissions at the Stutzman Center are Native Americans. A pillar of the addictions treatment approaches at the Center is, of course, Alcoholics Anonymous. But Native people find a culture-friendly AA during their stay in the Freedom Way Program. Using the principle that *culture is treatment,* the Medicine Wheel and the 12 Steps approach fit right in.

Valerie Staats (right) and another participant hold an honoring award during Hoop Journey IV on the Tuscarora Nation in New York State in 2003

Valerie Staats describes the blending of Native culture with AA and the cognitive component of recovery offered by the Wellbriety programs saying, *"For many, establishing contact with cultural activities helps our Native clients still the profound loneliness and shame they often carry. Reading the more current and accurate historical perspectives normalizes the despair and isolation many Natives have felt; it provides a cognitive life raft on which they can begin to express their fears and hopes."* The Freedom Way program is a landmark example of the Indianization of AA now taking place for Indian people in a manner unimaginable in the early 1950's when Native Americans started attending AA.

Hoop Journey II was a turning point of the Wellbriety Movement in the year 2000 (Peniska, Sr., 2001). The over-4000 mile walk, run and drive from Los Angeles to Washington, DC was dedicated to sobriety, recovery and an end to domestic violence in Indian communities. Even the White House noticed. Then Vice President Al Gore said, *"I am pleased to have this opportunity to send greetings to everyone gathered in Nashville for the two conferences of the Sacred Hoop Journey,"* in a letter of support received on June 10, 2000. A core group of about 25 Journeyers took the Hoop to numerous communities, both Native and non-Native, on a southern route across the country. At times, the core group swelled to 100 or more walkers as the Hoop was carried into a city or town. Eleven conferences were convened in selected towns or communities along the way featuring local people and Elders dedicated to wellness, as well as offering speakers from afar who talked about one or another subjects of Indian healing. A local coordinator helped bring the Hoop and its entourage into each community along the way. At all locations, the coming of the Hoop excited the community.

Kenny Winans, a Native American and the Arkansas Hoop Journey coordinator, speaks from the heart about the coming of the Hoop to his state on May 19, 2000:

"When we headed out to Fort Smith, the sky was grey and looked certain to rain, but we knew that the Great Spirit wouldn't let it because we had to bring the Sacred Hoop into Arkansas. We missed our exit and had to go into Oklahoma and turn around. When we came upon the walkers, just then the sky cleared. We knew it was going to be a good day. We talked to John White Shirt, one of the core Walkers, for a moment and went back to Arkansas to park the truck. Then Chief Jim Henson (United Keetoowah Band) came and

picked us up and took us to the transfer site. As we waited, the runners and walkers came in one by one off the road and greeted all that were at the site. When time came, the Hoop was brought out and smudged. And then we all smudged individually. All the while I kept a prayer: **Grandfather, let us do this in a good way that will please and glorify you.**

"I was not prepared for the overwhelming feeling I felt when we accepted the Hoop. I could feel the Great Spirit in the Hoop. I could feel the hope, the love, the strength, the prayers, the tools for recovery, and the cries of our ancestors. As the Hoop was being handed over by the Oklahoma people, Chief Henson said a prayer. We walked across the Arkansas bridge singing because our hearts were full of joy and pride. It was a good day. When we got over the bridge, we held the Hoop high and gave our war cries. Then we went to the park and handed the Hoop to the walkers as Chief Henson gave another prayer. When the ceremony was over, we sat around and visited with old friends and new friends. We look forward to the Hoop being in our state, and we look forward to the future."

Hoop Journey II (2000) began in Los Angeles on April 2 and concluded on July 9 and 10, 2000 in Washington, DC. In Washington, there was a great ceremony attended by hundreds at the Iwo Jima Memorial on July 9. The next day was filled with ceremonies, talks, and a closing Powwow. Hoop Journey II saw Native American leadership come out for sobriety and Wellbriety publicly, perhaps for the first time at a national level. Susan Masten, then President of the National Congress of American Indians (NCAI) took a brave step when she said, *"NCAI provides the forum for tribal leaders to set priorities on a national scale. I will work with you to carry your message of Wellbriety to the leadership at the National Congress of American Indians. ...As president of the National Congress of American Indians, I stand ready to assist in this effort to break the cycle of abuse and addiction. I ask that you keep me and your elected officials in your prayers so that we may bring honor to all of our people and so that we may have the strength and courage to walk in Wellbriety and assist in bringing a vision for healthy communities free of addiction and abuse."*

Kevin Gover, Pawnee, then Assistant Secretary of Indian Affairs, also threw his support to Native wellness as head of the BIA (Bureau of Indian Affairs). He said, *"Congratulations to those of you who have made all or any part of the Journey and thank you for the work that you are doing, for carrying the message of sobriety and wellness to a people who are in desperate need of it. ...In our daily work in the Bureau we deal with all these so-called big issues: Indian gaming, water rights, sovereignty, taxation and so on; but in the end none of them, none of them, is as important as this issue of wellness and sobriety in our communities."*

Hoop Journey II was a watershed event in a Movement filled with many turning points. It brought the message of Wellbriety to grassroots Indian people thirsty for it, as well as to Washington policy makers. It fed naturally into the National Wellbriety Month celebrations, which took place that September, and it firmed up the commitment for Hoop Journey III, which would follow in 2002. It also fed a desire for the various Wellbriety Programs and learning resources under development at White Bison and elsewhere. Appearances by Native American leaders such as Susan Masten and Kevin Gover were a statement that the tradition of resistance to alcohol that was present in the indigenous communities of North America since European contact was still alive. Now it was crystallizing around the Wellbriety Movement.

Mom and children at
a Wellbriety event

Susan Masten (L), then President of the NCAI, and Kevin Gover, then Assistant Secretary of Indian Affairs, Department of the Interior, were two Native American leaders who came forward in support of Wellbriety at the Hoop Journey Conference in Washington, DC in July of 2000.

Left, Hoop Journey II walkers at the Iwo Jima Memorial in Washington DC. Ira Hayes, Pima, is the historic figure at the far right of the statue. He is shown below in a 1943 photo. Below, left, youth from Hayes's community in Arizona dance at the Hoop Journey event in 2000. Hayes photo courtesy National Archives

Hoop Journey II--2000

2001-2002: The Wellbriety Movement Strengthens and Stabilizes

The next two years saw a strengthening and stabilization of the Wellbriety Movement in both the grassroots and nationally based arenas. By early 2001, some 38 Firestarters circles were taking place in 15 states. Firestarters were trained within their local or regional communities in three-day training sessions. Training consisted of the Medicine Wheel and the 12 Steps program, plus how to blend in local indigenous culture with the learning commitment. The Native community in Bishop, California became a strong Firestarters center. Here is how Leslie Davis from Bishop spoke of it. She said, *"Way back in 1998 one of our community members stopped by with a bunch of video tapes. He said our own treatment program in Bishop might benefit from them. I viewed the tapes and said Wow! They were the Medicine Wheel and the 12 Steps for men. We hadn't yet seen the women's videos. I watched the videos before I took the Firestarters Training in Sacramento. I'm a certified drug and alcohol counselor at the Toiyabe Indian health project and felt it might work for our community. This would have been the first time a program like this was tried."*

The year 2001 also saw the White Bison website take on the role of an easily accessible source of information about the Wellbriety Movement. Wellbriety! Online Magazine began regular publication on the website at that time, and has been going ever since. In September, 2001, the SAMHSA National Alcohol and Drug Addiction Recovery Month outreach event found a partner in National Native American Wellbriety Month; the partnership still continues. The emphasis of the September national outreach celebration in both the Native and non-Native communities that year was *putting a new face on recovery.* This meant that an individual, or a community, could be proud of being in recovery from chemical addictions. It meant that the hard work of addictions recovery should not be stigmatized, but rather welcomed and celebrated.

The Second Annual Circles of Recovery Conference opened in Rapid City, South Dakota that September to a premiere of the Hoop

Journey documentary video. *"You have an opportunity to heal in the next few days,"* Theda New Breast, Blackfeet Nation, told a gathering of over 200 people on that Thursday night in Rapid City, South Dakota. Ms. New Breast, a program provider for Native American healing for many years, facilitated discussion after the group premiered the moving video "Healing of a Nation" at the White Bison Strengthening our Families Conference. Most people had a hard time keeping a dry eye as the video recounted two of the White Bison cross country Hoop Journeys, one in 1999, and another in 2000. Viewers were silent as the video replayed a 911 domestic violence call, which was part of the family violence presentation in Phoenix, Arizona on the second Journey of the Sacred Hoop in 2000. They laughed when one of the Hoop journeyers clowned in the documentary as the L.A.-to-Washington event slowly walked, ran and drove the 100 Eagle Feather Hoop towards Washington in the spring and summer of 2000. By the end of the conference, over 450 attendees participated in the Strengthening Our Families Conference despite uncertain flight schedules and national grief over the September 11, 2001 events.

The next year, 2002, was a landmark year for Wellbriety. Hoop Journey III began on June 1 in Billings, Montana, traveling some 7000 miles through 16 cities West of the Mississippi river with the focus of Healing Women and Children. The Indianization of AA-related programs took another step forward when the Hoop came to Albuquerque on July 5, 2002. It was in Albuquerque on Hoop Journey III that Al-Anon forged a closer tie with Native Americans. During the Albuquerque Hoop Journey visit, Don Coyhis announced a Native-style Al-Anon event to take place later in the year. He said, *"Training will take place for people of all four directions on the Medicine Wheel and the 12 Steps and using the Native American approach within Al-Anon for their members who choose to participate in this aspect of the program."* Hoop Journey 2002 concluded in Denver on July 27.

The third Circles of Recovery Conference opened in Billings, Montana in late September 2002 to yet another premiere documentary video—this time of Hoop Journey III. Focused on strengthening communities, many new Wellbriety resources and alliances were introduced in Billings. To start with, for the first time ever there was representation from the federal government's drug and alcohol treatment and prevention efforts, as well as from CADCA, the Community Anti Drug Coalitions of America. SAMHSA's Dr. H Westley Clark, the ONDCPs (Office of National Drug Control Policy) Mary Ann Solberg, Henry Lozano, representing the President's Commission for Drug Free communities, and CADCA's General Arthur Dean all attested to the fact that Indian Country had Washington's attention and assistance in dealing with Native alcohol and other drug issues. The Wellbriety Movement is facilitated by White Bison, but other alliances for Wellbriety, distinct from White Bison, were developing, in keeping with the Indian tradition of resistance to intoxicating substances since Contact.

The Billings Conference also saw introduction of the new book, The Red Road to Wellbriety: In the Native American Way, which for the first time offered a culture-specific learning approach to the 12 Steps of Alcoholics Anonymous (White Bison, 2002). Also called the "Indian Big Book," this new publication took Native Americans through the 12 Steps, while at the same time offering 18 personal alcohol and other drug recovery stories told by Native American People. The book follows closely the revered Big Book of AA with the addition of chapters including information on codependency, Children of Alcoholics, and Family healing issues. The Red Road to Wellbriety is the first culture-specific rendering of the AA approach outside the original Alcoholics anonymous program; it also serves as a possible model for other ethnic groups desiring to customize AA's approach to their own ways. With the publication of The Red Road to Wellbriety, the Indianization of AA took yet another step forward. As a testimonial to the benefits that a culture-specific AA can bring, a Native American using the book said,

> *"Although I am in my 13th year of sobriety, I struggled with (standard 12 Step programs) because I could not relate or connect spiritually. Creator was not involved. It was*

through my connection and involvement with the American Indian Health Center that I was gifted a copy of the White Bison book, <u>The Red Road to Wellbriety in the Native American Way.</u> I read, eagerly awaiting the next word until I finished the book in a very short time. Each story, each word, touched the core of my being and my heart opened up in a way it never had before. I felt connected to the words. It was very powerful. This is what we need to lessen the number of relapses. This is what we need to hold the hearts and reach the spirits of the people."

Many other Wellbriety programs were introduced in Billings that year. Both Sons of Tradition and Daughters of Tradition (Simonelli, 2001) were publicized at the Billings Conference. Both programs are addiction prevention learning approaches for Native American Youth. Billings also saw presentation of The Wellbriety for Youth program under Jeri Brunoe Samson (Warm Springs Nation), and Wellbriety For Prisons under Blaine Wood (Cherokee). Theda New Breast gave a workshop on the popular Native American GONA (Gathering of Native Americans) program, which had allied itself with the Wellbriety Movement after years of its own grassroots acceptance (New Breast, 2004). The Sacred Buffalo Robe which had been a long standing symbol of NANACOA (National Association of Native American Children of Alcoholics) and the 100 Eagle Feather Hoop were paired in a ceremonial coming-together event at the Billings Conference. This ceremonial connection cleared the way for the revitalization of NANACOA, which had been such a strong force in Native healing since the late 1980's but had grown dormant in recent years. The Third Annual Circles of Recovery Conference in 2002 was a great exposition for still further expansion of the Wellbriety Movement to come in 2003 and 2004.

2003-2004 "A Minefield of Miracles"

Hoop Journey IV began in Cherokee, North Carolina on April 9, 2003 and concluded over a thousand miles later on May 23 in Oneida, Wisconsin. In between, thousands of participants in more than 16 communities or unplanned stops east of the Mississippi River experienced the Hoop and the Journey's wellness presentations especially for Native men and children (Well Nations, 2003). By 2003, the Wellbriety Movement was reaching out to both Native and non-Native people.   A visit to Ground Zero, the September 11 site in lower Manhattan on April 17, 2003, was an offering of the Hoop's gift of Forgiving the Unforgivable to the world at large (Simonelli, 2003).

The July-August, 2003 issue of Well Nations Magazine features photos of a Hoop Ceremony held at the World Trade Center site in Lower Manhattan on Hoop Journey IV. Well Nations Magazine, published by Lakota Kevin Peniska, Sr., is another example of the vitality of the American Indian/Alaska Native wellness movement in North America.

One of the exceptional happenings that day was the inclusion of Sergeant Hardy and Lt. Kevin Devlin of the New York and New Jersey Port Authority Police Department into the Circle that formed as part of the healing ceremony. *"I spend more time with my co-workers than I do with some members of my family, so the loss was deep,"* said Lt. Devlin, remembering many of his co-officers who died there on September 11. Both police officers were smudged with sage and participated in the healing circle that followed.

Above, a scene from the start of Hoop Journey IV in Cherokee, NC in April of 2003. Right, Glenn Funmaker is honored with a miniature Hoop at the close of the Hoop Journey in May of 2003 on the Oneida Nation in Wisconsin

Hoop Journey IV made its final visit of 2003 to the Oneida Indian Reservation at Oneida, Wisconsin. The coming of the Hoop to Oneida was part of the three-day Oneida Sobriety Conference, marking another landmark in the many bridges between Native culture and Alcoholics Anonymous. At this conference from May 23-25 of 2003, the Oneida Nation was celebrating a fifty-year anniversary as the first Native American AA group. Glenn Funmaker, Oneida, a coordinator of the Oneida Conference, speaks of the connection between Alcoholics Anonymous and the Oneida Nation in Wisconsin. *"The Oneida Sobriety Conference Committee is made up of people in recovery who are part of an AA group called* the Hobart Indian Group," he said. *"That particular group is the first Native American AA group in the country. There were four founding members who established that group in Oneida at the Parish Hall 50 years ago. Their names are Lester Skenadore, Arthur Skenadore, Howard Elm, and Van Roy Thomas. We honor them. The group died out 3 or 4 times over the years but what they had back then sustained us and kept us going. The group refuses to die. Now been going again for 5 years once again."*

The Oneida Conference demonstrated that the Indianization of AA leaves both the heart of Alcoholics Anonymous and the heart of Native culture intact. It proves what Native Americans began to learn as they started to attend AA in the early 1950's and what the Indian Big Book says: *"Time and again our Elders have said that the 12 Steps of AA are just the same as the principles that our ancestors lived by, with only one change. When we place the 12 Steps in a circle then they come into alignment with the circle teachings that we know from many of our tribal ways."*

The Fourth Annual Circles of Recovery Conference took place in Albuquerque, New Mexico in September of 2003. The 2003 Conference was dedicated to healing and strengthening Indian Nations. With this fourth Conference, the Medicine Wheel sequence of healing and strengthening Individuals, Families, Communities and Nations, in that order, had come full circle. The multicultural tradition of the Circles of Recovery Conferences was strong once again with representatives from all four directions in attendance. SAMHSA's's director Dr. H. Westley Clark was back in support of Native recovery from alcohol and other drugs. In his National Alcohol and Drug Recovery Month, September 2003 talk at the Conference he brought greetings from the governmental addictions recovery effort in America. *"It is important for us to celebrate Recovery Month in as many different settings as possible,"* said Dr. Clark. *"Today's observance is one of more than 215 community events scheduled around the country celebrating National Alcohol and Drug Addiction Recovery Month. ... I want to salute all of you who have taken your time to sit in this room today. Your commitment to this process is what has motivated me to get on a plane and come here today. I thank White Bison for its role in convening the Fourth Annual Circles of Recovery Strengthening Our Nations Conference in Albuquerque. White Bison has been a pioneer in helping American Indians identify what works best to combat drug and alcohol addiction. Through these efforts and vital linkages, and advocacy, we can have a sustained strategy to assist and partner with American Indians and Alaska Natives."*

The guidance of Native Elders, which had begun with that visit to New Mexico in 1984 resulting in the Four Laws of Change, was still alive almost 20 years later in 2003. Wellbriety Elders Horace Axtell, Ozzie Williamson and Bill Iron Moccasin hosted two Elder's panel discussions late in the afternoons of September 19 and 20. Many conference participants turned out to ask questions and to hear answers from life experiences stretching back into the 1940's. Bill Iron Moccasin spoke about his own remembrances of the Indian boarding school legacy. He said, *"Our parents went to boarding school and passed it on to us. The disciplinarian I went to school under was a graduate of Carlisle. He was one of the meanest guys I ever met. He would really bat us around and he was a Native American. He did it to us because that's how they treated him at Carlisle Indian School. This kind of behavior is not part of our culture. It's a learned behavior from the other society, the other culture."*

Many people who had connected with the Wellbriety Movement by way of the grassroots Firestarters Circles in Indian communities from across North America visited with each other during the 2003 conference.

The coming of 2004 saw 600 trained Firestarters participating in 300 local Firestarters Circles in Native American communities. Two different Daughters of Tradition Programs serving girls from the ages of 8 to 17 years old were staffed by 75 trained DOT facilitators with 2500 DOT kits disseminated to Indian country. The Sons of Tradition Program for Native boys ages 13-17 was beginning to train facilitators and would go on to teach culture-based prevention to at-risk youth. The White Bison website continued to serve as a communication hub for the Wellbriety Movement with hits achieving more than an impressive 185,000 per week. The Wellbriety for Prisons Program was steadily setting up prison Firestarters Circles for incarcerated Native Americans. White Bison's alliance with SAMHSA in the name of the Wellbriety Movement was proving effective as 2000 Children of Alcoholics kits, especially designed for Native Americans, were made available free of charge in February of 2004. Over 100 participants in the Native community of Juneau, Alaska undertook the first "Seven Trainings" integrated community-healing program in March. And in April, a three day training event designed to teach Native community leaders about Wellbriety coalition building in their home communities took place in Denver, Colorado.

A Daughters of Tradition Honoring Dinner was held for girls and their families at the American Indian Center in Chicago in April of 2004. The girls received shawls for their commitments and good work as part of the Daughters of Tradition program

The Seven Trainings approach provides continuity and connectedness for the Wellbriety movement because a broad spectrum of the Native community's healing needs is met by seven simultaneous training sessions during a three-day period. The coalition building curriculum is important because it teaches diverse communities how to link up and present themselves as one unified movement for indigenous healing and wellness—the Wellbriety Movement. Wellbriety for Prisons is especially important because it provides hope for indigenous people incarcerated in a system that does not understand them. It also reveals that when Native People begin their healing journey in prison they often go on to provide a very powerful wellness resource for their communities after release. Wellbriety for Youth is important because, to quote an old saying, "An ounce of prevention is worth a pound of cure." Addictions prevention knowledge goes a long way for young people. It's well known in the Wellbriety Movement now that there are many Native American youth who have never tasted alcohol or used drugs. There is also a move now to take the grassroots Firestarters program to the indigenous people of Australia through a series of dialogs and online distance learning through the White Bison website. When this happens, the local indigenous Aboriginal cultural orientation in Australia will take the place of the North American Medicine Wheel approach, but they probably won't be too far apart.

A Vision for the Future

To support the Wellbriety Movement, the current vision of the White Bison organization is to see 100 communities into healing by the year 2010. How will this come about? The Wellbriety Movement is a distributed, decentralized phenomenon spread throughout North America. It's not a top-down structure. *"We look at all of this as a web,"* says Don Coyhis. *"...we don't look at it as an organization with an org chart, we look at it like a web of interconnectedness using the Internet, the wire that goes all over the world. The information and the teachings of the Wellbriety Movement that are available on our website are freely shared with all people,"* he says.

Those who have been trained as Firestarters often utilize their skills in ways that best fit the recovery and healing needs of their own local communities. They are one force to realize the 2010 vision. *"As a result of the Firestarters groups, we now have circles of wellness activities that have sprung up in many of the communities,"* says Coyhis. *"Those centers in the communities are expanding."*

Jackie Red Woman Lindow, Ottawa Nation, is a Firestarter who, with her husband Kelly, hosts regular wellness get-togethers at their 12 acre farm in Wisconsin. She uses her Firestarter training to enhance what she and Kelly have done in the past. She says, *"Our door is always open to people who need us. Through the years, hundreds of people have come to camp, enjoy our bonfires, talk, and enjoy the peace and healing of our beautiful Waushara County land. It's not always those who are abusing alcohol who have come for help. Some who are diagnosed with cancer have come here; and once we had an 11-year old boy who was beating up his mother. Everyone is 'recovering' from something and needs healing."*

Maria Barrera, a Latina and member of the Anahuac people of Mexico has taken Indian ministry into federal prisons in the Washington, DC area for many years. Her Firestarter training increased her skill to provide for Native Americans in prison. She explains, *"One of the things that I am now able to bring to any community—it doesn't matter whether it is African American, Latino, Asian etc—one of the things that the Firestarters training and the Wellbriety Movement did for me was to actually help me connect more with my own spiritual being. ...Now, when I come to talk to people, the main and most important thing that I try to bring above all is my spirituality. I help people with intergenerational trauma gain internal peace. If you have that internal peace you can deal with many things."*

The *Warrior Down* concept was introduced at the Fifth Annual National Wellbriety Conference in Denver, Colorado in April, 2005. When operational, Warrior Down will place a safety net under those who have returned from treatment programs or other residential alcohol and drug rehabilitation activities to their own home communities. Trained community Warrior Down volunteers will provide a caring and capable group of people to keep an eye on and help returnees if they are having trouble maintaining their own sobriety program. This is a vision for the future that may also have much to offer communities everywhere.

"We are walking in a minefield of miracles!" Don Coyhis exclaimed when Hoop Journey II pulled into Albuquerque, New Mexico on April 21, 2000. *"Every day on this Walk there are many opportunities to walk in the minefield of miracles. We see so much*

proof that the Creator is involved in this walk. When we start to get well we become really aware of the gifts of our ancestors. The best intervention, treatment or recovery program is our culture," he said on that day during the Hoop Journey.

The Wellbriety Movement continues to be a miracle of community mobilization for Native American healing. It is an active force for positive change in Indian country as well as a model that may be emulated outside Native culture. The Movement carries with it the First Nations tradition of resistance to alcohol since first contact and goes beyond with a brand new opportunity for American Indian and Alaska Native societies to create a healthy and prosperous future. The Wellbriety Movement is just beginning.

A Vision for the Future

Youth (left) take a bow after presenting a skit entitled, "We're Eagles, Not Chickens!" at the Wellbriety Conference in Denver in 2005. Don Coyhis (right) greets participants at the Conference. The vision for a future of well, prosperous and thriving American Indian and Alaska Native people in Turtle Island, the Native name for North America, is in the capable hands, minds and hearts of the Youth. May Creator smile on us all.

References

New Breast, T. (2004). Sobriety and American Indian history (continued), *Well Nations Magazine,* November, December, 2004, pp 15-19

Peniska, Sr., K. (2001). Don Coyhis: A man. His vision. The Sacred Hoop. *Well Nations Magazine,* January, February, 2001, pp 48-52

Simonelli, R. (2001,Winter). Daughters of Tradition: An educational program for girls in the age group of 9-12, *Winds of Change,* 16(1) pp 18-20

Simonelli, R. (2003). Healing at Ground Zero, *Well Nations Magazine,* July-August, 2003, pp. 48-49

Well Nations, (2003). Lessons from the old culture: A Well Nations interview with Bill Iron Moccasin, *Well Nations Magazine,* March-April, 2003, pp 40-42

White Bison, Inc. (1998). *The Medicine Wheel and the 12 Steps for Women.* (Video) Colorado Springs, Colorado: White Bison

White Bison, Inc. (2002). *The Red Road to Wellbriety: In the Native American Way.* Colorado Springs, Colorado: White Bison, Inc.

Part Four: **The Lessons of History**

American Indians experienced massive losses...in a long legacy of chronic trauma and unresolved grief across generations. This phenomena...contributes to the current social pathology of high rates of suicide, homicide, domestic violence, child abuse, alcoholism and other social problems among American Indians.

—Maria Brave Heart & L. Debruyn

Native Americans occupy Alcatraz Island in San Francisco Bay in the late 1960's. A period of social activism and militancy signaled the re-empowerment of Native North America, a step towards healing intergenerational trauma.
Photo credit Ilka Hartmann

Chapter Fifteen

Addiction, Recovery and the Processes of Colonization and Decolonization

Few works on Native American alcohol problems have placed alcohol problems and their solutions within their proper historical context—a context that is fundamentally about the processes of colonization and decolonization (Duran and Duran, 1995). In exploring this context, we are guided by Patricia Morgan's (1983) observation that alcohol plays a significant role in establishing and sustaining patterns of domination and subordination between groups of people. Such patterns are established and maintained by:

- shaping perceptions of alcohol's effects on particular groups of people,

- promoting alcohol intoxication to dissipate political protest and maintain a group's subjugated status,

- paternalistically controlling the supply of alcohol, and

- asserting mechanisms of social control behind the rationale of controlling alcohol problems.

There are many predictable patterns in the evolving relationship between colonizing and colonized cultures, and alcohol and other drugs play a significant role in these relationships. While our focus in this final discussion will be on the principles underlying the role of alcohol in the colonization and decolonization of the Indigenous Peoples of North America, the processes we will describe are very similar to broader relationships with culturally subjugated groups within North America (See Helmer, 1975) and throughout the world. For example, please also see McKnight, 2002 for a description of the outcome of such processes in an Australian Aboriginal community.

Drugs and Cultural Conquest

Part of the process of colonization (cultural conquest and domination) is the replacement of the celebrated drugs of the colonized with the celebrated drugs of the colonizer.

In the beginning of our story, Native tribes integrated psychoactive drugs within their tribal cultures in ways that protected individuals and benefited the tribe. The drug choices and the rituals that surrounded them varied, but reflected the most basic values and beliefs of each tribe. The rituals surrounding the use of these drugs provided a protective shield against injury to the individual and the tribe. The European assault on Native cultures included the banishment (of hallucinogens) and theft (commodification and commercialization of tobacco) of Native drugs and the forced injection of distilled alcohol into Native cultures. These processes of banishment, theft and infusion were part of the larger assault on Native history, culture, language and folkways.

Problem Development

Alcohol-and other drug-related problems (and other health and social problems) rise in tandem with the family and cultural breakdown that follows subjugation and the loss of ancestral traditions.

We have documented that significant alcohol-related problems rose among American Indian and Alaska Native tribes only when these tribes came under physical and cultural assault and when alcohol shifted from a token of intercultural contact to a tool of economic, political and sexual exploitation. Promoting patterns of drug consumption among the colonized serves the long-term interests of the colonizer by providing an instrument of manipulation, anesthetizing misery and fostering an escapist alternative to political protest. The management of psychoactive drugs is the prerogative of the cultural elite (Stauffer, 1971); the designation of particular drugs as *good* or *bad* and defining vulnerability for alcohol and other drug problems to particular groups of people is an exercise of cultural power and control.

Problem Attribution

During periods of intercultural conflict, differences in alcohol or other drug use patterns between the colonizer and the colonized are 1) noted or fabricated; 2) exaggerated; and 3) framed in euphemisms of superiority and inferiority.

Intoxication by members of the colonizing culture is defined as a personal prerogative and, in excess, a problem of personal pathology; intoxication by members of the colonized culture is universally defined in terms of group pathology (biological and cultural inferiority).

The mythology of racial vulnerability to alcohol or other drug problems is part of a larger body of ideas and beliefs that dehumanize and objectify those being subjugated. The colonizer offers stories of drunkenness, addiction, vice and violence that are plagued by overgeneralization (from individual to tribe and from one tribe to all tribes), misinterpretation, and myths. These ideas are weapons that serve the colonizer's cultural, economic, political and religious interests (Berkhofer, 1979; Andersen, 1988). By portraying alcohol or other drugs as a function of racial inferiority, by portraying all Native alcohol problems within the clinical framework of alcoholism and by portraying alcoholism as the primary source of crime, violence, insanity, disease, and social disorder, the colonizer escapes culpability for the processes of colonization from which these very problems flow. Such ideas are crucial to the process of colonization. Memi explains:

> *The colonized are weak and incapable of self-governance and thus need the protection and authority of the colonizer. The colonized are lazy and thus require the goading of the colonizer. The colonized are liars and thieves and thus require the surveillance of the colonizer. The colonized are savages whose violence is contained only by the firm control of the colonizer. The colonized are primitive and backwards and thus require the civilizing hand of the colonizer. The colonized are wretched and ungrateful for the benefits that the colonizer bestows upon them. The colonized are prone to drunkenness... All this is for one purpose: One does not have a serious obligation to an animal or an object* (Memi, 1957, p. 86).

Solution Framing

The problems arising within colonized peoples are defined as unresolvable within these communities and solvable only through the patronage of the dominant culture.

While such patronage is a means of expiating the guilt of the oppressor by reframing that role to one of benefactor, it also serves other purposes. The patronage of the colonizer is delivered through values, assumptions, and methods that further disempower the colonized, displace indigenous leaders and weaken indigenous institutions.

Indoctrination of the Colonized (Internalized Oppression)

It is not sufficient to cultivate these views (alcohol problems as a product of racial taint) among the colonizers; such views must also be inculcated within the colonized.

As Freire (1970, p. 151) has noted, "For cultural invasion to succeed, it is essential that those invaded become convinced of their intrinsic inferiority." By transmitting the firewater myths within Native communities, Native People were given a collective template defining and predicting their own destiny. To accept the myth as truth was to court a path of potential destruction. To declare the Indian an alcoholic by racial birth was as insidious a weapon as the repeating rifle and smallpox-infected blankets. Oppressors do not have to kill all of the oppressed; through the power of prophecy, they can teach them to kill themselves.

Richard Thatcher in his landmark study of the impact of firewater myths on communities of First Nations in Canada explains:

> *...this construct* [firewater mythology] *has, in effect, acquired a life of its own, becoming an independent cause of destructive substance use patterns and an obstacle to personal and community self-determination and resiliency. (p. 116)....*[the firewater mythology] *guides the drinking patterns of socially disaffected tribe members, implicitly justifies drunken episodes, and serves as an excuse for drunken comportment" (Thatcher, 2004, p.130).*

Social Control

Over time, alcohol and other drugs serve as tools of sustained pacification.

Such pacification is achieved through active promotion of drug availability (or passive tolerance of drug trafficking), channeling the emotional roots of potential political protest into personal dissipation and self-destruction, and using alcohol and other drug-related problems as a rationale for external social control. The portrayal of drug-related problems as contagious provides a further rationale for sequestering individuals and whole communities and injecting agents of colonial control within Native communities.

Drug Use as Protest

External efforts by the colonizer to suppress or control drug availability imbues the drug with meaning as a symbol of cultural protest and sets up acts of defiant self-destruction (Lurie, 1974).

This replaces real protest (acts of physical, political, economic and cultural opposition) with acts of personal dissipation and cultural destruction. The most cunning thing the white man ever did was to convince Indians that the white man did not want the Indians to drink alcohol. The inevitable acts of defiant drunkenness constituted not acts of protest, but acts of personal and cultural suicide.

Internalized Rage

Oppressors do not have to kill all of the oppressed; by inculcating racial self-hatred, they can teach them to kill each other. Dempsey (2002, p. 147) vividly describes how this process works in his description of the impact of cultural demoralization and the whiskey trade on the Blackfoot.

> *They lived for the moment when alcohol carried them into a delirium of intoxication.... Their aggressions, once directed towards their enemies, now pointed inward towards their own people. They were easily offended, often reacting to an innocent comment or action with such violence that death or permanent injury was the inevitable result. They drank, they argued, they fought, they killed* (Dempsey 2002).

Therapeutic and Cultural Revitalization Movements

Indigenous movements emerge that provide a solution to alcohol-related problems (and other health and social problems) through processes of personal purification and cultural renewal.

These movements are Nativist (desiring the expulsion of alien persons and customs), pan-Indian (intertribal), revivalist (seeking restoration of lost customs), vitalistic (incorporating selective elements of the alien culture), messianic (seeing salvation in a human divinity), mellenarian (forseeing an apocalyptic end of suffering and the arrival of new or lost world), introversionist/therapeutic/redemptive (providing a framework for the reconstruction of personal health and identity) (Wallace, 1956; Voget, 1956; Aberle, 1966). These are multidimensional movements, and their power can be found in this very characteristic. The movements we have described have religious, political and cultural dimensions, and all were therapeutic in that they offered a framework for personal recovery/healing and the transformation of personal identity and interpersonal relationships.

Context for Emergence

Abstinence-based healing and cultural revitalization movements emerge during times of extreme personal hardship and cultural crisis (Linton, 1943).

New healing movements will emerge when new problems arise among peoples under physical and cultural assault that cannot be addressed by existing rituals of healing (Garrity, 2000). The prophetic movements, for example, were acts of cultural resistance that grew out of the apocalypse of epidemic diseases, military assaults, loss of ancestral lands, geographical displacement, disruption of tribal economies, and starvation. Native tribes faced what Wallace (1956) has christened the "threat of mazeway disintegration"--the complete obliteration of their view of themselves and the world. Native alcoholics "hit bottom" as the cultures in which they were nested also were "hitting bottom." Any solution for the former had to also offer hope for the latter. Where traditional tribal cultures lacked specific beliefs or healing ceremonies to treat alcohol problems, new beliefs and healing rituals arose that specifically addressed these problems and the larger context in which they were emerging. The call for rejection of alcohol as an act of personal redemption was mirrored by the call for the rejection of Anglo-American folkways and the embrace of ancestral folkways as acts of cultural redemption.

Problem Redefinition

New cultural revitalization and healing movements redefine the source and nature of alcohol problems.

Cultural renewal movements reclaim indigenous history and retell the history of colonization from their own perspective, including new liberating understandings of problems that arose during and after colonization. Paulo Friere describes such a breakthrough of consciousness in the words of a Chilean peasant:

> *They used to say we were unproductive because we were lazy and drunkards. All lies. Now that we are respected as men, we're going to show everyone that we were never drunkards or lazy. We were oppressed!* (Friere, 1970, p. 50).

Framing Native alcohol problems solely in terms of individual maladaptations to contemporary circumstances ignores the soil--the history and policies--from which these problems grow. There is an ecology of Indian alcohol problems that is ignored in models that define their etiology in terms of personal vulnerability (Thatcher, 2004). The movements described here rejected the attribution of Native alcohol problems solely in terms of the biological vulnerability of a race or of individuals, and instead defined the emergence of alcohol problems in terms of the cultural disintegration that accompanied European assault of Native tribes and the subsequent policies of the U.S. government that undermined the foundations of personal and tribal health. Native peoples within these movements viewed alcohol as a sickness that could manifest itself in mental, physical and spiritual forms. The alcohol sickness, like all sickness, was thought to result from disharmony in the spiritual world and in the relationship between the individual and the community and between the tribe and the outside world. In this view, the root source of alcohol sickness could lie in one's own behavior or be rooted within the actions and misdeeds of others. In the worldview of the eighteenth and nineteenth centuries, Native religious and cultural revitalization movements, the spiritual, the cultural and the historical were so interconnected as to be synonymous (Avery, 1991). These views are being rekindled in contemporary models that view alcohol and other drug problems as intergenerational products of historical trauma (Brave Heart & DeBruyn, 1998; Brave Heart, 2003).

Alcohol or other drug intoxication can be framed in terms of self-medication of *anomie*—alienation from society due to societal instability or loss of social and moral values in that society. Such self-medication may anesthetize the trauma of personal/cultural loss, but it can also be understood in terms of violence against self and one's own culture. The very essence of colonization is programming the colonized to destroy themselves and their own kind. The portrayal of colonized people as posing a threat of violence to members of the dominant culture belies the fact that most acts of lethal violence by the colonized are acts of cultural fratricide or suicide. In this light, the refusal to kill oneself or one's cultural brothers or sisters is an act of resistance—an act of liberation.

The successful resolution of alcohol and other drug problems in Native communities is contingent upon how accurately those problems are defined. The successful resolution of these problems today requires that they first be fundamentally redefined (Thatcher, 2004). That will require viewing Native alcohol problems in the context of transcultural learning (drinking patterns initially learned from non-Indian people), historical trauma and the self-fulfilling internalization of the drunken Indian stereotype, rather than viewing such problems through the framework of disease and racially-defined biological vulnerability.

Solution Framing

Abstinence-based Native American cultural revitalization movements shift the locus of the solution to Native alcohol problems from resources outside to resources within Native communities and from a focus on the individual to a focus on the community.

When Eduardo and Bonnie Duran declare that "the answer to the problem of alcohol existed and continues to exist within the Native American community" and Andy Chelsea of the Shuswap Tribe in Alkali Lake declares, *"The community is the treatment center,"* they are reflecting this change in orientation. The contention that alcohol problems cannot be solved by tribes themselves rests on an assumption of the inferiority of Native cultures and provides a rationale for federal control of Indian tribes and federal intrusion into the lives of individual Indians. Today's new initiatives (e.g., the Healthy Nations Initiative) rest on the assumption that Native communities, with appropriate resources, have the internal knowledge and capabilities to resolve their own substance-related problems and that such solutions can only come from within these communities (Noe, Fleming & Manson, 2003).

Medical models that posit the source and solution of alcohol problems within the individual may be unsuitable for the resolution of Native alcohol problems (Duran and Duran, 1995; Beauvais and LaBoueff, 1985). In this cultural context, the individual and the community are inseparable. Out of this inseparability comes the deep involvement of family and the community in alcoholism healing rituals, whether through their participation in the sacred dances or through offering prayers for the one seeking support for his or her continued sobriety. Native therapies, such as those utilized by the Navajo, prescribe healing rituals through which the person who had been made sick by offended spirits could be returned to health. These rituals often portray or symbolize death and rebirth and alienation from and re-connection with family and community. Where the treatment of the alcoholism in Western medicine often involves a period of isolation of the alcoholic from family and community, the treatment of alcoholism in Native traditions involves physically and spiritually surrounding the alcoholic with family and community (Nofz, 1988). The growing integration of traditional teachings and rituals into Native alcohol treatment programs reflects this principle (Mills, 2003).

Native frameworks of recovery from alcoholism have always been framed in terms of hope for the individual and hope for a community and a people as a whole. These differences--individualistic versus collectivist views--of alcohol problems and their resolution constitute an enormous gulf in white and Native understandings and approaches to alcohol problems (Wing and Crow, 1995; Holmes and Antell, 2001). The movements we have reviewed in this book reinforce the idea that for a besieged people, the personal health (recovery) of the wounded individual is inseparable from the personal health (recovery) of the tribe. Having undergone their own personal transformation, the messianic leaders of these movements conveyed systems of belief and rituals through which their disciples and followers could undergo similar transformations, and in the process incited a process of cultural transformation. Part of this transformation was a shift from clan and tribal identities to a more encompassing, collective designation of Native tribes as "the People" engaged in a struggle for their very existence against the forces of Euro-American colonization.

No framework of recovery for Native alcoholism has sustained itself that focused ONLY on the individual. As noted in the recently published *Red Road to Wellbriety,*

> *The Wellbriety of the community creates a healing sanctuary--a culture of recovery--for the wounded individual, just as the growing Wellbriety of the individual feeds the strength of the community. The individual, family and community are not separate; they are one. To injure one is to injure all; to heal one is to heal all* (White Bison, Inc., 2002, p.f).

It may be that insight about the necessity for healing the individual and the community *simultaneously,* applying to indigenous or tribal peoples, will prove essential to the healing of non-indigenous societies as well—especially when addictions rates rise to high (pandemic or epidemic) proportions.

Chapter 15 · Part 2

Kinetic Ideas and Closing Reflections

A tipi on Alcatraz Island. Leaders of the occupation in
1969 met in this tipi to consider government offers and
to plan responses during the action that helped to begin
Native American re-empowerment. Golden Gate Bridge
and San Francisco Bay are in the background.
Photo Courtesy of the National Park Service.

Kinetic Ideas

_____ resound from the abstinence-based cultural
_____ation movements we've explored. The first is that *recovery
is a reality in the lives of hundreds of thousands of Indian People.*
These movements offer living proof of what modern research is
confirming:

1. Native Americans as a whole have higher abstinence
   rates than the U.S. population in general (Lemert, 1982).

2. Fifty percent of the Native American men and 20% of the
   Native American women who abstain from alcohol
   identify themselves as recovered alcoholics (Whitacker,
   1982).

3. With increased education and stable employment, many
   Natives migrate from patterns of problematic binge
   drinking toward a controlled pattern of alcohol
   consumption (Lemert, 1982).

4. Many Native Americans achieve long-term stable
   sobriety (Moss, et al, 1985).

The second message is *there are many pathways to recovery
within Native communities.* These pathways may include mutual aid
frameworks (e.g., the "Indianization of Alcoholics Anonymous"),
religious pathways of recovery (from Christianity to Native
religions), and cultural frameworks (the "Red Road") of recovery.
Curley (1967), in his study of Mescalero Apache drinking patterns,
noted that involvement with the Apache Assembly of God church
was one of the primary ways that formerly heavy drinking Apache
men achieved sobriety. There is also evidence that many Native
Americans abandon problematic relationships with alcohol without
formal assistance. Thomas Hill (1974) in his study of the alcohol
problems among the Winnebago found many Native American
males assumed the role of "hell-raiser" in their transition out of
adolescence but later assumed adult responsibilities ("settling down"

into the role of "family man")--a transition marked by the shift from destructive binge drinking to abstinence. This pattern of problem resolution via developmental maturation, confirmed by recent epidemiological studies of Indian communities (Bezdek, Croy, Spicer, et al, 2004), suggests a culturally-prescribed pathway of what research scientists refer to as spontaneous remission, natural recovery, or maturing out of alcohol problems.

Recovery, Revitalization and Decolonization

A significant milestone in decolonization is the development of language and ideas within Native cultures to describe the individual and collective problems that resulted from cultural domination. The religious and cultural revitalization movements described in these pages offered their own understandings and interventions into alcohol and other drug problems. These movements conveyed to a subjugated people that they had a right to exist--to be seen as they choose to present themselves and have their experiences and problems expressed in words and stories of their own creation. These words and stories conveyed a singular message: cultural enmeshment and cultural identity constitute protective shields against and instruments of healing for alcohol and other drug-related problems among Native Peoples—a proposition that is finding increasing support in the scientific literature (Westermeyer and Neider, 1985; Whitebeck, Chien, Hoyt & Adams, 2004; Spicer, 2001).

Wounded Healers

Another consistent theme of the early revitalization movements is that *those healed from alcoholism became healers called to heal others similarly afflicted.* Jilek (1971), in a study of modern Native healers, confirms that such healers entered these roles via ecstatic (experiential) initiation rather than didactic (formal education) initiation. In this pattern, one acquires the power and obligation to assist in the healing of others upon one's own healing (Slagler and Weibel-Orlano, 1986; Jilek, 1978a). The religious and revitalization movements described here provided an opportunity, in healing oneself, to heal the family and community as well.

Shared Elements

There are many shared themes within the prophetic movements. First, many of these movements began with the near-death/rebirth or dream/vision experience of someone usually not noted for their religious inclinations or their leadership abilities. *The transformed life of the prophet offers visible proof of the legitimacy of the spiritual encounter, and provides a model for similar life-transforming conversion experiences among the followers.* Drawn from the experiences of the prophet were teachings, songs, and dances that were to be spread to other Native Peoples. The messages themselves often predicted the cataclysmic end of the white world, a renewal of Native tribes and the return of the dead (both people and animals). In preparation for this new era, Native Peoples were admonished to prepare themselves via ritual purification (isolation, fasting, and purging), sobriety, participation in traditional dances and ceremonies, and moral living. Such promises of renewal and resurrection elicited great hope among peoples who had lost or were losing everything and everyone dear to them. The death of so many children was particularly devastating and the promise of imminent re-unification with loved ones was a powerful siren call to grieving survivors (Vibert, 1995; Kracht, 1992).

Perhaps most important for the theme of this book, each of the revitalization movements demonized alcohol and drunkenness, elevated sobriety to an act of personal healing and cultural resistance, and wrapped sobriety in a larger moral code of living. Healing and morality are inseparable within these movements (Voget, 1956). The cure of physical/spiritual illness is inseparable from what one believes and how one's life is conducted. It is in this integration that one finds the essence of the difference between Western and Native medicine. Ernie Benedict, a Mohawk elder, describes:

> *The difference that exists is that the White doctor's medicines tend to be very mechanical. The person is repaired but he is not better than he was before. It is possible in the Indian way to be a better person after going through a sickness followed by the proper medicine* (Benedict and Porter, 1977, Quoted in Jilek, 1978a).

The new moral code was reinforced within new sobriety-based social relationships and social activities. Abstinence-based cultural revitalization movements provided new esteem-infusing roles. From the "holders" within Handsome Lake's recovery circles to the "Road Chief" and "Water woman" of the peyote ritual to the "headman" and "elders" of the Indian Shaker Church to the "singers" and "pledges" in the Sun Dance or the "drum keeper" and "whip man" in the Gourd Dance, these movements placed people in roles that re-affirmed their value. Such roles accrue to the direct participants and to other members of the tribe who support such ceremonies, e.g., seamstresses, cooks, hosts.

The movements described here provided a framework for expressing strong emotion--grief, anguish, rage, guilt, gratitude—and anchored new beliefs and sentiments in sacred rituals, sacred texts, sacred objects, and sacred places (Slagler and Weibel-Orlano, 1986). What cultural revitalization movements offered and still offer is not an escapist retreat into the past, but the reinterpretation of traditions and beliefs to meet the challenges of contemporary Native life. The survival of these movements hinges on how well this synthesis works at both personal and tribal levels. Cultural frameworks of recovery incorporate elements of traditional belief and ceremony while re-interpreting and adding new elements to those beliefs and ceremonies that have meaning to the individual and the tribe. These movements don't so much call on a return to ancestral traditions as call for an application and re-interpretation of those teachings and traditions in response to contemporary realities. They provide a vehicle to prevent alcohol problems, a venue for personal recovery from alcohol problems, and systems of belief

h an oppressed people can restore their dignity and
direction for their lives (Jilek, 1978a ; McLoughlin,
1,..

Identity Reconstruction

Another element of historical significance is that *Native sobriety-based movements defined all aboriginal tribes of the Americas as a single People sharing a collective fate in their struggle for survival against Anglo-American encroachment.* This bold stroke sought to replace traditional tribal rivalries with an intertribal identity. Some even went beyond this boundary to see the world in terms of color and whiteness. William Apess, for example, proclaimed:

> *If black or red skins or any other skin of color is disgraceful to God, it appears that he has disgraced himself a great deal–for he has made fifteen colored people to one white and placed them here upon this earth* (Quoted in Haynes, 1996, p. 9).

Culture as Treatment

Cultural revitalization movements use culture as an instrument of healing. The Native leaders depicted in this book did not tell their followers that they were biologically vulnerable to the disease of alcoholism. They told them that alcohol problems were a symptom of their loss of culture. They told them that Indian People had lost their minds when they lost their culture and that there would be no sanity or sobriety without a retrieval and revitalization of those cultures. That approach takes on added significance in light of Westermeyer and Neider's (1986) ten-year study of the relationship between cultural affiliation and recovery from alcoholism. They report two major findings. First, those with the highest degree of cultural affiliation at intake had the highest recovery rates when assessed ten years later. Second, cultural affiliation changed through the stages of recovery. Many of the Native Americans who successfully recovered from alcoholism reduced cultural affiliation during their first year of recovery (as a means of breaking ties with pro-drinking relationships), but then increased cultural affiliation as their sobriety strengthened. Wilson & Hart, 2004 have recently confirmed the role of ethnic identity and spirituality in Native American recovery from alcoholism. In perhaps the most definitive study of the effects of cultural affiliation on the resolution of alcohol problems among American Indians, Spicer (2001, p. 238) concluded that "transformations of the self and its relationship to core symbols in a particular cultural system of meaning appear to lie at the heart of how people are restored to wholeness following their problematic involvements with alcohol."

These studies confirm that cultural affiliation is a crucial dimension of recovery, but is not, by itself, a panacea for the resolution of alcohol problems. Cultural affiliation is not the solution to addiction where alcohol and other drug use is culturally pervasive and abstinence is socially unacceptable. Cultural affiliation is an antidote for addiction when there exists strong social support for abstinence and recovery within one's cultural community. This suggests that, as cultures of recovery grow within Native communities, cultural affiliation will become an ever-widening pathway of personal and family recovery. This further underscores why interventions into Native alcohol problems must be at the tribal level as well as the individual level.

Suppression

The response of the colonizer (dominant society) to Native religious and cultural revitalization movements is a story of active and sustained suppression. Fanon (1963) has vividly described the response to decolonization movements:

> *Decolonization never takes place unnoticed, for it influences individuals and modifies them fundamentally. It transforms spectators crushed with their inessentiality into privileged actors, with the grandiose glare of history's floodlights upon*

them. It brings a natural rhythm into existence, introduced by new men, and with it a new language and a new humanity. Decolonization is the veritable creation of a new man...the "thing" which was colonized becomes a man during the same process by which it frees itself (Fanon, 1963, pp. 36-37).

The suppression of Native American cultural revitalization movements has included physical and verbal attacks on Native prophets; ridicule and condemnation of the "Indian Preachers;" criticism of the Indian Shaker Church (Collins, 1950); and the legal suppression of Peyotism, the Ghost Dance and the Sun Dance (Hertzberg, 1971; Lawson and Scholes, 1986). In the earliest history of these movements, it is quite clear that sober Native leaders and their sober tribes posed more of a physical and political threat to white encroachment than did those individuals and tribes neutered by the disorganizing effects of alcohol. Sober leadership, the dissolution of traditional tribal rivalries and the emergence of intertribal coalitions collectively constituted the most significant threat to the conquest of the Indigenous Peoples of North America.

Fate of Revitalization Movements

Some of the sobriety-based Native movements catalogued in this chapter were short-lived. They were ultimately overwhelmed by the same forces of cultural dissolution that had spawned their birth. As one reviewer of these movements noted, "some failed, not through any deficiency and execution, but because circumstances made defeat inevitable" (Wallace, 1956, p. 275). *What constitutes a remarkable story of resiliency is the survival of some of these movements.* Considering that none of the culturally dominant nineteenth century alcoholism recovery support structures (the Washingtonians, the fraternal temperance societies, the reform clubs) survived as therapeutic movements, it is noteworthy that the Handsome Lake Religion, the Indian Shaker Church and the Native American Church continue to operate in much the same way they did more than a century ago. They provide ideological and social support for Native recovery from alcohol problems and alcoholism today as they did more than a century ago. The job of the leaders of these early movements was to maintain generational momentum, and the existence of a strong and spreading Wellbriety Movement in Indian Country today is evidence that these leaders helped us get to this day.

Care must be taken in extolling the achievements of early Native American recovery pioneers that similar achievements of today's recovery leaders remain untold. Vine Deloria, Jr. (1969,1988), has noted the toll such reification can exact by inadvertently conveying to contemporary Native People that they are only a physically and culturally diluted remnant of a once noble race of Super-Indians. The leaders of the cultural revitalization movements—then and now—are remarkable individuals, but remarkable because they exemplify the resilience of Native People. These movements and their leaders sustained the hope of a people in ways that transcend the life of each movement and the life of each leader. The first task of a colonized people is to survive, and these movements played important roles in such survival. Each movement, each generation of leaders, refined and transported a message of sobriety that made future movements possible. That process continues today.

Closing Reflections

The untold story we have shared is important to Native People, but it is also important to all Americans. The construction of Native alcohol and other drug problems set a model that would be applied to other colonized or disenfranchised peoples within American history–, e.g., the drinking provisions in the Slave Codes, the anti-opium (anti-Chinese) campaign of the 1870s, the association between blacks and cocaine in the late 19th century, the exploitation of anti-Catholic and anti-German sentiment during the drive for legal prohibition of alcohol, the role of anti-Mexican sentiment in the

Marihuana Tax Act of 1937, etc. (Taylor, 1931; White, 1978; Musto, 1973).

The story of the destructive effects of alcohol and alcoholism among Native Peoples has been often noted, but this is a tale filled with mistruths that served, and continue to serve, particular cultural and political interests. We have tried to deconstruct some of these misconceptions while acknowledging the devastating role alcohol has played in the history of many Native tribes. But most importantly, we have sought to convey that this story is not one of passive injury but instead one of active and prolonged resistance and recovery. There are continual voices of Native recovery from the early Woodland prophetic traditions of the eighteenth century through the nineteenth century messianic movements of the trans-Mississippi region to twentieth century sobriety-based, cultural revitalization movements and the rising Wellbriety Movement.

We have described a variety of cultural responses to alcohol problems in Native America. All rejected alcohol and provided a framework for personal recovery from alcohol-related problems and alcoholism. Today, reaffirmation of traditional beliefs and ceremonies, participation in Native A.A. groups and Native religions (e.g., the Native American Church or Indian Shaker Church), or participation in an evangelical Christian church continue to provide frameworks through which Native People initiate and sustain recoveries from alcohol problems and alcoholism (Weisner, Weibel-Orlando, and Long, 1984).

This review illustrates the enormous diversity of abstinence-based religious and cultural revitalization movements that provide personal and cultural solutions to alcohol problems both within and across Native tribes. These movements constitute the first geographically decentralized sobriety-based support structures in North America (and probably the world), and mark the first efforts to frame personal sobriety within the larger context of the physical and cultural survival of a people.

The story we have told is as contemporary as it is historical. The processes described continue to unfold and mark enduring rhythms in the relationship between Native and Anglo cultures. Many of the surviving movements continue to provide indigenous frameworks for alcoholism recovery. The echoes of yesterday are heard in contemporary cultural approaches to alcoholism treatment/recovery. Treatment settings are incorporating Native purification and healing practices (sacred dances, the sweat lodge, and talking circles) (Hall, 1985; May, 1989) for Native People suffering from alcoholism who have also been estranged from tribal identity, language, and ceremonies. And there is the Wellbriety Movement in Indian Country that is tapping many of the deepest recovery traditions we have reviewed. Cultural pain requires cultural healing. The alcohol that has flowed in Indian Country is the blood of a wounded people. Alcohol could not have flowed so freely if the body of Indian life had not been so grievously wounded. These losses must be grieved and the wounds must be cauterized.

The key tasks of cultural revitalization movements are to:

1) preserve ancestral language, ideas, histories, art, and ceremonies, and

2) to interpret these elements within each generation in ways that promote personal and tribal health.

These traditions must be preserved in their original form so that they may be re-interpreted in eras to come. Alcohol problems are not an indigenous element of Indian culture. They are a malignant cancer that was injected into a healthy culture with the intent of poisoning and killing a culture and its people. Seen in the context of this history, sobriety is a revolutionary act--a refusal to participate in the destruction of oneself and one's culture.

While alcoholism has constituted and continues to constitute a serious health problem in many Native communities, any report on Native alcoholism lies by omission if it withholds the story of Native recovery. The evidence of that recovery can be found in nearly all Native communities and on the pages of a growing body of scientific studies that are documenting high rates of alcoholism recovery among Native People (Leung, et al, 1993). Particularly encouraging are efforts such as The People Awakening Project—a collaboration between Alaskan Native and the University of Alaska to document pathways to sobriety within Alaskan Native communities. This book is not just a call for change; it is an acknowledgement that such change is already underway. We want to emphasize and reaffirm that alcoholism recovery is alive and well in North American Indian Communities and has been for more than 250 years!!

TO ALL OUR RELATIONS!

References

Aberle, D.F. (1966). *The Peyote Religion among the Navaho.* Chicago: Aldine Publishing Company.

Anderson, T.I. (1988). *Alaska Hooch.* Fairbanks, AK: Hoo-Che-Noo.

Avery, C. (1991). Native American medicine: Traditional healing. *Journal of the American Medical Association 256*(17):271-273.

Beauvais, F. & LaBoueff, S. (1985). Drug and alcohol abuse interventions in American Indian communities. *The International Journal of the Addictions. 20*(1):139-171.

Berkhofer, R. (1979). *The White Man's Indian: Images of the American Indian from Columbus to the Present.* New York: Vintage.

Bezdek, M., Croy, C., Spicer, P & the AI-SUPERPFP TEAM (2004). Documenting natural recovery in American-Indian drinking behavior: A coding scheme. *Journal of Studies on Alcohol,* July, pp. 428-433.

Brave Heart, M.Y.H. (2003). The historical trauma response among Natives and its relationship with substance abuse: A Lakota illustration. *Journal of Psychoactive Drugs,* 35(1), 7-13.

Brave Heart, MY.H. & DeBruyn, L.M. (1998). The American Indian Holocaust: Healing historical unresolved grief. *American Indian and Alaska Native Mental Health Research,* 8(2), 56-78.

Collins, J. (1950). The Indian Shaker Church. *Southwestern Journal of Anthropology. 6:*403-412.

Curley, R.T. (1967). Drinking patterns of the Mescalaro Apache. *Quarterly Journal of Studies on Alcohol, 28:*116-131.

Deloria, V., Jr. (1969, 1988). *Custer Died for Your Sins.* Norman: University of Oklahoma Press.

Dempsey, H. (2002). *Firewater: The Impact of the Whiskey Trade on the Blackfoot Nation.* Calgary: Fifth House Ltd.

Duran, E. and Duran, B. (1995). *Native American Postcolonial Psychology.* Albany: State University of New York Press.

Fanon, F. (1967). *Black Skin, White Masks.* New York: Grove Weinfeld.

Fanon, F. (1963). *The Wretched of the Earth.* New York: Grove Press.

Freire, P. (1970, 1992). *Pedagogy of the Oppressed.* New York: Continuum.

Freire, P. (1985). *The Politics of Education.* New York: Bergion and Garvey.

Garrity, J. (2000). Jesus, peyote, and the holy people: Alcohol abuse and the ethos of power in Navajo Healing. *Medical Anthropology Quarterly, 14*(4):521-542.

Hall, R. (1985). Distribution of the sweat lodge in alcohol treatment programs. *Current Anthropology, 26*(1):134-135.

Haynes, C. (1996). The formation of Methodist and Pequot identity in the conversion narrative of William Apess. *Early American Literature, 31*(1):25-44).

Helmer, J. (1975). *Drugs and Minority Oppression.* New York: Seabury Press.

Hertzberg, H. (1971). *The Search for an American Indian Identity: Modern Pan-Indian Movements.* Syracuse, N.Y.: Syracuse University Press.

Hill, T.W. (1974). From hell-raiser to family man. In: Spradley, J.L. and McCurdy, D.W. Eds., *Conformity and Conflict: Readings in Cultural Anthropology* 2nd, ed/. Boston: Little Brown & Company, pp. 186-200.

Holmes, M and Antell, J. (2001). The Social construction of American Indian drinking: Perceptions of American Indian and white officials. *The Sociological Quarterly, 42*(2):151-173.

Jilek, W.G. (1971). From crazy witch doctor to auxiliary psychotherapist--the changing image of the medicine man. *Psychiatria Clinica, 4*:200-220.

Jilek, W.G. (1978). Native renaissance: The survival of indigenous therapeutic ceremonials among North American Indians. *Transcultural Psychiatric Research, 15*:117-147.

Kracht, B.R. (1992) The Kiowa ghost dance, 1894-1916: An unheralded revitalization movement. *Ethnohistory, 39*(Fall):452-477.

Lawson, P.E. and Scholes, J. (1986). Jurisprudence, peyote and the Native American Church. *American Indian Culture and Research Journal, 10*(1):13-27.

Lemert, E.M. (1982). Drinking among American Indians. In: Gomberg, E.L., White, H.R., and Carpenter, J.A., Eds., *Alcohol, Science, and Society Revisited.* New Brunswick, NJ: Rutgers Center of Alcohol Studies, pp. 80-95.

Linton, R. (1943). Nativistic movements. *American Anthropologist, 45:*230-240.

Lurie, N. (1974). The world's oldest on-going protest demonstration: North American Indian drinking patterns In: Hundley, N. Ed. *The American Indian.* Santa Barbara, California: CLIO Books, pp.55-76

May, P. (1989). That was yesterday, and (hopefully) yesterday is gone. *American Indian and Alaska Native Mental Health Research, 2*(3):71-74.

McLoughlin, W.G. (1990). Ghost dance movements: Some thoughts on definition based on Cherokee history. *Ethnohistory, 37*(Winter):25-44.

McKnight, D. (2002). *From Hunting to Drinking: The Devastating Effects of Alcohol on an Australian Aboriginal Community.* New York: Routledge.

Memi, A. (1957, 1991). *The Colonizer and the Colonized.* Boston: Beacon Press.

Mills, P.A. (2003). Incorporating Yup'ik and Cup'ik Eskimo traditions into behavioral health treatment. *Journal of Psychoactive Drugs,* 35(1), 85-88.

Morgan, P. (1983). Alcohol, disinhibition, and domination: A conceptual analysis. In *Alcohol and Disinhibition: Nature and Meaning of the Link,* Ed. by Room and Collins. Washington D.C.: U.S. Government Printing Office.

Moss, F., Edwards, E.D., Edwards, M.E., Janzen, F.V., and Howell, G. (1985) Sobriety and American Indian problem drinkers. *Alcoholism Treatment Quarterly, 2*(2):81-96.

Musto, D. (1973). *The American Disease: Origins of Narcotic Controls,* New Haven, CT: Yale University Press.

Noe, T., Fleming, C & Manson, S. (2003). Health Nations: Reducing substance abuse in American Indian and Alaskan Native communities. *Journal of Psychoactive Drugs,* 35(1), 15-25.

Nofz, M.P. (1988). Alcohol abuse and culturally marginal American Indians. *Social Casework* 69(2):67-73.

Slagle, L. and Weibel-Orlando, J. (1986). The Indian Shaker Church and Alcoholics Anonymous Revitalistic curing cults. *H u m a n Organization,* 45(4):310-319.

Spicer, P. (2001). Culture and the restoration of self among American Indian Drinkers, *Social Science & Medicine,* 53: 227-240.

Stauffer, R. (1971). *The Role of Drugs in Political Change.* New York: General Learning Press.

Taylor, P.S. (1931). *Mexicans in the United States. Report of the Wickersham Commission: Crime and the Foreign Born.* Washington, D.C.: U.S. Government Printing Office.

Thatcher, R. (2004). *Fighting Firewater Fictions: Moving Beyond the Disease Model of Alcoholism in First Nations.* Toronto: University of Toronto Press.

Vibert, E. (1995). "The natives were strong to live": Reinterpreting early-nineteenth-century prophetic movements in the Columbia Plateau. *Ethnohistory, 42*(Spring):197-229

Voget, F. (1956). The American Indian in transition: Reformation and accommodation. *American Anthropologist* 58:249-63.

Wallace, A. (1956). Revitalization movements. *American Anthropologist* 58:264-281.

Weisner, W.S., Weibel-Orlando, J.C., & Long, J. (1984). "Serious drinking," "White man's drinking" and "teetotaling": Drinking levels and styles in an urban American Indian Population. *Journal of Studies on Alcohol,* 45(3), 237-250.

Westermeyer, J & Neider, J. (1986). Cultural affiliation among American Indian alcoholics: Correlations and change over a ten year period. *Annals of the New York Academy of Science 472*:179-188.

Westermeyer, J. &Neider, J. (1984). Predicting treatment outcome after ten years among American Indian alcoholics. *Alcoholism: Clinical and Experimental Research, 8*(2):179-184.

Whitaker, J.O. (1982). Alcohol and the Standing Rock Sioux Tribe: A twenty-year follow-up study. *Journal of Studies on Alcohol 43*(3):191-200.

Whitbeck, L.B, Chien, X, Hoyt, D.R., & Adams, G.W. (2004). Discrimination, historical loss and enculturation: Culturally specific risk and resiliency factors for alcohol abuse among American Indians. Journal of Studies on Alcohol, July, pp. 409-418.

White Bison, Inc. (2002). *The Red Road to Wellbriety: In the Native American Way,* Colorado Springs, Colorado: White Bison, Inc.

White, W. (1979). Themes in chemical prohibition. In *Drugs in perspective.* Rockville, MD: National Drug Abuse Center/National Institute on Drug Abuse.

Wilson, T.L. and Hart, K.E. (2004). Abstinence self-efficacy among Native American inpatients attending treatment for alcoholism. Paper presented at the 2004 Convention of the Association for the Advancement of Behavior Therapy, November, New Orleans.

Wing, D.M. and Crow, S.S. (1995). An ethnonursing study of Muscogee (Creek) Indians and effective health care practices for treating alcohol abuse. *Family and Community Health 18*(2):52-64.

Appendix One

The Jefferson-Handsome Lake Letter

This famous letter from the third President of the United States, Thomas Jefferson, to Handsome Lake, Seneca, is included in order to place Handsome Lake's life and times into an historical context. The letter also demonstrates the different orientation and values of the American system when compared with indigenous society.

Washington, November 3, 1802

TO BROTHER HANDSOME LAKE:

I have received the message in writing which you sent me through Captain Irvine, our confidential agent, placed near you for the purpose of communicating and transacting between us, whatever may be useful for both nations. I am happy to learn you have been so far favored by the Divine spirit as to be made sensible of those things which are for your good and that of your people, and of those which are hurtful to you; and particularly that you and they see the ruinous effects which the abuse of spirituous liquors have produced upon them. It has weakened their bodies, enervated their minds, exposed them to hunger, cold, nakedness, and poverty, kept them in perpetual broils, and reduced their population. I do not wonder then, brother, at your censures, not only on your own people, who have voluntarily gone into these fatal habits, but on all the nations of white people who have supplied their calls for this article. But these nations have done to you only what they do among themselves. They have sold what individuals wish to buy, leaving to every one to be the guardian of his own health and happiness. Spirituous liquors are not in themselves bad, they are often found to be an excellent medicine for the sick; it is the improper and intemperate use of them, by those in health, which makes them injurious. But as you find that your people cannot refrain from an ill use of them, I greatly applaud your resolution not to use them at all. We have too affectionate a concern for your happiness to place the paltry gain on the sale of these articles in competition with the injury they do you. And as it is the desire of your nation, that no spirits should be sent among them, I am authorized by the great council of the United States to prohibit them. I will sincerely cooperate with your wise men in any proper measures for this purpose, which shall be agreeable to them.

You remind me, brother, of what I said to you, when you visited me the last winter, that the lands you then held would remain yours, and shall never go from you but when you should be disposed to sell. This I now repeat, and will ever abide by. We, indeed, are always ready to buy land; but we will never ask but when you wish to sell; and our laws, in order to protect you against imposition, have forbidden individuals to purchase lands from you; and have rendered it necessary, when you desire to sell, even to a State, that an agent from the United States should attend the sale, see that your consent is freely given, a satisfactory price paid, and report to us what has been done, for our approbation. This was done in the late case of which you complain. The deputies of your nation came forward, in all the forms which we have been used to consider as evidence of the will of your nation. They proposed to sell to the State of New York certain parcels of land, of small extent, and detached from the body of your other lands; the State of New York was desirous to buy. I sent an agent, in whom we could trust, to see that your consent was free, and the sale fair. All was reported to be free and fair. The lands were your property. The right to sell is one of the rights of property. To forbid you the exercise of that right would be a wrong to your nation. Nor do I think, brother, that the sale of lands is, under all circumstances, injurious to your people. While they depended on hunting, the more extensive the forest around them, the more game they would yield. But going into a state of agriculture, it may be as advantageous to a society, as it is to an individual, who has more land than he can improve, to sell a part, and lay out the money in stocks and implements of agriculture, for the better improvement of the residue. A little land well stocked and improved, will yield more than a great deal without stock or improvement. I hope, therefore, that on further reflection, you will see this transaction in a more favorable light, both as it concerns the interest of your nation, and the exercise of that superintending care which I am sincerely anxious to employ for their subsistence and happiness. Go on then, brother, in the great reformation you have undertaken. Persuade our red brethren then to be sober, and to cultivate their lands; and their women to spin and weave for their families. You will soon see your women and children well fed and clothed, your men living happily in peace and plenty, and your numbers increasing from year to year. It will be a great glory to you to have been the instrument of so happy a change, and your children's children, from generation to generation, will repeat your name with love and gratitude forever. In all your enterprises for the good of your people, you may count with confidence on the aid and protection of the United States, and on the sincerity and zeal with which I am myself animated in the furthering of this humane work. You are our brethren of the same land; we wish your prosperity as brethren should do. Farewell.

(Signed)

Thomas Jefferson

Courtesy, The Avalon Project at Yale Law School

Available on the World Wide Web at:

http://www.yale.edu/lawweb/avalon/jeffind2.htm

Appendix 2

The Good Mind

Excerpted from a Talk by Freida Jacques, Onondaga Nation,
given at the Gathering of Native American Men,
Pike National Forest, Colorado
May 31, June 1-2, 1996

Discipline of the Good Mind

Thousands of years ago, at a time when our people were in the midst of wars and pervasive violence, the Peacemaker came and brought us a message of love and peace. One of the gifts he brought to us at that time was the concept of the Good Mind (Ganigonhi:yoh). As children grow up in our Nation they hear the words "use a good mind", many times. I felt that a deeper explanation of what using the Good Mind means would be beneficial and this is how I explain it.

When the Europeans first came to this continent they were surprised to see that the Haudenosaunee did not have a police force or many laws to encourage good behavior in the people. I feel that the use of Ganigonhi:yoh was so pervasive that it was unnecessary to have a police force and many laws.

I refer to the Good Mind as a discipline, rather than just a description of a person's state of mind. First of all Ganigonhi:yoh recognizes that we are connected to the good, that we have access to a loving source of good thoughts. Each and every one of us has many, many thoughts each day. With discipline we can become aware of each thought, see its substance, realize its intent, and then determine if you should follow and build on that thought. This realization that you have a will over your thinking is key. You have a choice to follow your thoughts based on a loving purpose (the Good Mind) or let go of thoughts and certainly not build upon thoughts steeped in anger and judgment. In most cases it takes thousands of thoughts to get to a point where you are harboring hate for someone and capable of violence. This discipline helps us redirect our thinking to more constructive, kind and loving thoughts. Since our actions follow our thoughts, what we are doing with our lives will be kinder and gentler. Since the words we speak follow our thoughts, we also have a way of affecting the world around us with words that will reflect the Good Mind.

By observing our thoughts we may begin to identify areas in our lives that may need to be reflected upon and healed. Watch out for over reactions to your experiences and also under-reactions for they may help identify places that need healing. Consider being more willing to look at these parts of yourself and seek out people who work as healers to help you work through old hurts and anger. Stifled anger never goes away. It lingers in the background ready to show up to add to your next angry moment. This can make for more dramatic moments than you may want. Work through old anger and life will be less painful.

While we actively become aware of our thoughts, especially those that have a kind and loving intent, we naturally allow ourselves to become spiritually in tune with the Creator's wishes. This allows us to use our talents to fulfill our purpose on Earth. This is my motivation to follow the Good Mind. When it is time to leave this

Earth I would like to feel that I fulfilled the purpose that the Creator sent me here to accomplish.

As Haudenosaunee, we give thanks to all the parts of Creation that make life possible here on Earth (The Ganonhanion). This keeps us connected with the very vital purpose of all living things. So our respect and love includes all parts of Creation. This understanding helps us use the Good Mind in our interactions with the natural world around us.

It has been said many times that change begins with the individual. If you want change to happen, begin by changing yourself. The discipline of the Good Mind is a process anyone can use to help him or herself change. Much can be accomplished with prayer, love and patience.

About the Authors

Don L. Coyhis

Don Coyhis, Mohican Nation, is a member of the Stockbridge-Munsee tribal nation of Wisconsin. He Founded White Bison, Inc. in 1988 and has brought programs for Native American healing to tribal communities for over 15 years. He is the author of the four-book set, <u>Meditations with Native American Elders</u>. His articles about Wellbriety and cultural healing have appeared in Winds of Change, Counselor, Well Nations, and Child Welfare.

William L. White

Bill White is a Senior Research Consultant at Chestnut Health Systems and author of <u>Slaying the Dragon: The History of Addiction Treatment and Recovery in America</u>. His articles detailing the history of recovery among Native American tribes have been published in Well Nations, Addiction, Alcoholism Treatment Quarterly and Counselor.

Authors Don Coyhis (left), and Bill White sign copies of the first draft of this book, distributed to about 150 Native People for community feedback, which has been incorporated into this edition.

About White Bison, Inc.

White Bison, Inc. An American Indian Non-Profit {501(c)3} Corporation

White Bison was founded in 1988 by Don Coyhis, Mohican Nation, with the vision of achieving 95% sobriety among Native American youth by the year 2000. This was a brave challenge in those days because the facts about alcohol use and its effects in American Indian and Alaskan Native communities were grim. Throughout the late 1980's, and into the entire decade of the 90's White Bison created and offered training sessions, sobriety and addictions recovery programs, and diverse media resources to Native American communities throughout North America in pursuit of the Founding vision. White Bison facilitated the birth of the Wellbriety Movement during the last quarter of the 1990's. As the 21st Century dawned and the Wellbriety Movement had become well established, the White Bison organizational vision changed to become the dream of seeing 100 communities enter healing by the year 2010. In the spirit of this second vision, a community enters healing when individuals within a core group of the community begin to change in a good way, and when they begin to bring healing programs to the community so that their brothers and sisters might have a similar opportunity. White Bison's vision of the 100 Communities is strong and is taking place in Native American communities now.

Some of White Bison's healing outreach to indigenous North America since its Founding have included the following activities and resources:

National Gatherings

1990-Present: Regular presentations at the AISES (American Indian Science and Engineering Society) National Conferences

1994: Gathering of the Elders (Janesville, WI) *Dedication of the Sacred Hoop*

1995: Women's Leadership Gathering (Denver, CO)

1996: Gathering of Native American Men (Florissant, CO)

Sacred Hoop Journeys (*Video documentaries can be obtained from White Bison, Inc.*)

1999: Healing the Nations: Visits to 32 Tribal Colleges

2001: Wiping the Tears (Over-4000 mile walk, run and drive from Los Angeles to Washington, DC)

2002: Healing Native Women and Children (19 urban and reservation communities west of the Mississippi River)

2003: Healing Native Men and Children (17 urban and reservation communities east of the Mississippi River)

National Wellbriety Conferences

1999:	Strengthening Individuals (Colorado Springs, CO)
2001:	Strengthening Our Families (Rapid City, SD)
2002:	Strengthening Our Communities (Billings, MT)
2003:	Strengthening Our Nations (Albuquerque, NM)
2005:	Healing the Hurts: The Grassroots Speaks (Denver, CO)

Wellbriety Resources

1990:	Natural Path to Growth (personal development program)
1993:	*Meditations With Native American Elders* by Don Coyhis (4 book set)
1993:	The Healing Forest Program (a culturally-based community development program first presented for the Passamaquoddy Tribe, Maine)
1997:	The Medicine Wheel and the 12 Steps for Men (video and workbooks)
1998:	The Medicine Wheel and the 12 Steps for Women (video and workbooks)
1998:	Creation and Implementation of the **Circles of Recovery** Concept (Grassroots community circles at the center of community healing efforts)
1999:	*Understanding Native American Culture: Insights for Recovery Professionals* by Don Coyhis (booklet)

1999:   Firestarters Program (Culture-based grassroots community healing program)

2000:   *Wellbriety! Online Magazine* (www.whitebison.org)

2000:   Daughters of Tradition I (Culture-based prevention curriculum for girls age 8-12)

2001:   Firestarters––The Family Series (Strengthening our Families)

2002:   Sons of Tradition (Culture-based character building and prevention curriculum for boys age 13-17)

2002:   Medicine Wheel and the 12 Steps (For friends and families and adult children of alcoholics)

2002:   Children of Alcoholics (A support program for children of those impaired by alcohol abuse)

2002:   *The Red Road to Wellbriety: In the Native American Way* by White Bison, Inc. (a cultural 12 Step-based book of recovery support resources developed by and for Native Americans in recovery)

2002:   Wellbriety for Youth (Prevention and leadershp development for Native American youth)

2002:   Wellbriety for Prisons (A recovery support system for those returning from prison)

2003:   Families of Tradition (A recovery support curriculum for families that have experienced substance abuse)

2004:   Daughters of Tradition II (Character building and prevention education for girls ages 13-17)

2004:	7 Trainings (an integrated all-community program delivering a grassroots Wellbriety curriculum in a 3-day conference format)
2004	Coalition Building (A training program to unify those working in healing issues in their home communities)
2005:	Warrior Down (A relapse prevention and recovery support program for Native Americans)
2005:	*Alcohol Problems in Native America: The Untold Story of Resistance and Recovery–The truth about the lie* by Don Coyhis and William L. White. (a history book documenting Native American efforts to oppose alcohol since first European contact)

Accomplishments: Firestarters and the Circles of Recovery

1998-2005	Approximately 1500 certified Firestarters and nearly 800 Circles of Recovery nationwide
	Facilitation certification training for Firestarters (3-day, 3 evening intensive training)
	Programs, books and other resources mentioned in this listing are available from White Bison, Inc. Visit the website www.whitebison.org or call 1-877-871-1495 or 719-548-1000

We, at White Bison, invite each and every person inspired by what Native Americans are doing for themselves in healing and self-determination, with assistance from allies like yourself, to participate in the Wellbriety Movement. Visit www.whitebison.org or call 877-871-1495 or 719-548-1000 to learn more.

Index